Murder
on the
Baltimore Express

THE PLOT TO KEEP ABRAHAM LINCOLN FROM BECOMING PRESIDENT

SUZANNE JURMAIN

YELLOW JACKET

YELLOW JACKET

An imprint of Little Bee Books
New York, NY
Text copyright © 2021 by Suzanne Jurmain
All rights reserved, including the right of
reproduction in whole or in part in any form.
Yellow Jacket and associated colophon
are trademarks of Little Bee Books.
Photographs and other imagery were obtained from the
Library of Congress and the National Archives Catalog.
Manufactured in China   RRD 1220
First Edition 10 9 8 7 6 5 4 3 2 1
ISBN 978-1-4998-1044-8 (hc)
yellowjacketreads.com

Library of Congress Cataloging-in-Publication Data
Names: Jurmain, Suzanne, author. | Title: Murder on the Baltimore Express:
the plot to keep Abraham Lincoln from becoming president / Suzanne Jurmain.
Description: New York, NY: Yellow Jacket, an imprint of Little Bee Books, 2021.
Includes bibliographical references and index. | Audience: Ages 10-14
Audience: Grades 7-9 | Summary: "In February 1861 newly elected President Abraham
Lincoln set out on a triumphant 2,000 mile cross-country railroad trip that would take
him to his inauguration in Washington, D.C. At the same time, a band of fanatic southern
Confederate sympathizers decided to stop Lincoln from reaching Washington and taking
office. Furious because the new president's desire to end slavery threatened their way
of life, they devised a secret plan: Lincoln would be murdered by an assassin's bullet in
Baltimore. But as rushing railway trains carried Abraham Lincoln towards death, Detective
Allan Pinkerton learned of the plot—and set out to save the president. Dive into this
incredibly fun and suspenseful true story and learn what other history books never told you:
the secret of Lincoln's great escape" —Provided by publisher.
Identifiers: LCCN 2020047219 | Subjects: LCSH: Lincoln, Abraham, 1809-1865—
Assassination attempts—Juvenile literature. | Presidents—Assassination attempts—United
States—Juvenile literature. | Lincoln, Abraham, 1809-1865—Travel—Washington (D.C.) —
Juvenile literature. | Conspiracies—United States—History—19th century—Juvenile literature.
| Pinkerton, Allan, 1819-1884—Juvenile literature.
Classification: LCC E457.4.J87 2021 | DDC 973.7092—dc23
LC record available at https://lccn.loc.gov/2020047219

For information about special discounts on bulk purchases,
please contact Little Bee Books at sales@littlebeebooks.com.

For Theo,
who gives me hope for the future

Contents

♪ Timeline ♪

1619 The first African slaves are sold in Virginia.

1620-1700s The number of slaves grows rapidly in the South and much more slowly in the North.

1693 The first American pamphlet condemning slavery is published by a Pennsylvania Quaker. This officially begins the argument over whether or not slavery should exist in America.

1776 The Declaration of Independence frees the American colonies from England and declares "all men are created equal" and have a right to liberty. Some feel this means that there is no place for slavery in America and hope the practice will soon disappear.

1777 Some northern states, starting with Vermont, begin to ban slavery.

1788 Both northern and southern states accept the Constitution as the basic law of the land and join to form the United States of America. Because southerners are unwilling to join the new nation if they have to give up slavery, the Constitution does not ban it. Instead, each state is allowed to decide whether its citizens can legally own slaves.

1790s–mid-1800s Cotton becomes the South's most important product. Since this crop is grown by slaves, slavery becomes essential to southern prosperity.

1830s Activists in the northern states launch a campaign to end slavery. They say the practice is evil and demand that the U.S. government free all slaves and ban the practice immediately.

1837 A prominent southern senator declares that slavery is a "positive good." His opinion is shared by most other white southerners.

1840-1860 Slavery completely disappears in the North. More northerners decide slavery is a sin, and the movement to free all U.S. slaves grows rapidly in northern states.

1800-1860	As Americans move west, northerners and southerners fight—sometimes violently—over whether slavery should be allowed in each new state
NOV. 1860	Abraham Lincoln, a man who wants to end slavery, is elected U.S. president.
DEC. 1860–FEB. 1861	Fearing Lincoln and northerners might eventually ban slavery, seven southern slaveholding states cut their ties to the United States. They form their own nation—the Confederate States of America—with a constitution that declares slavery will never be banned.
FEB. 18, 1861	Former U.S. senator Jefferson Davis is sworn in as president of the Confederate States of America.
MAR. 4, 1861	Abraham Lincoln is sworn in as president of the United States. Because of slavery, America is now divided into two opposing nations. War between the North and South is predicted.
APR. 1861	Confederate soldiers attack Fort Sumter. Lincoln calls for troops to defend the Union, and the Civil War begins.
JAN. 1863	Lincoln strikes the first major blow against slavery by issuing the Emancipation Proclamation, which frees all slaves in the Confederate states.
NOV. 1864	Abraham Lincoln is reelected.
1864-1865	Abraham Lincoln urges Congress to permanently outlaw slavery in America by adding the Thirteenth Amendment to the Constitution.
APR. 1864	The U.S. Senate approves the Thirteenth Amendment.
JAN. 1865	The U.S. House of Representatives approves the Thirteenth Amendment.
APR. 9, 1865	The Civil War ends as Union forces defeat the Confederacy. The nation is reunited.
APR. 14, 1865	Abraham Lincoln is assassinated by a pro-slavery southerner.
DEC. 1865	The Thirteenth Amendment becomes law, and slavery is officially banned across the United States.

❧ The Principal Characters ❧
(in alphabetical order)

Robert Anderson
U.S. major commanding federal troops at Fort Sumter

David Bookstaver
New York City detective hired by General Winfield Scott to
investigate southern plots against Abraham Lincoln

John Wilkes Booth
actor and assassin

Harry Davies
agent working for the Pinkerton National Detective Agency

Jefferson Davis
president of the Confederate States of America

Dorothea Dix
famed human rights activist

Frederick Douglass
former slave, famous abolitionist crusader, and advisor to
President Lincoln

Samuel Felton
president of the Philadelphia, Wilmington,
and Baltimore Railroad

Cypriano Ferrandini
leader of a group conspiring to murder Abraham Lincoln

Hannibal Hamlin
U.S. vice president who served during Lincoln's first term

Otis Hillard
member of Ferrandini's group of conspirators

John Hutcheson
false name used by Allan Pinkerton when pretending to be
a southern secessionist businessman

Norman Judd
one of Abraham Lincoln's closest advisors

George P. Kane
chief of the Baltimore city police

Ward Hill Lamon
friend of Lincoln's who sometimes acted as
the president's bodyguard

Abraham Lincoln
sixteenth president of the United States

Mary Todd Lincoln
wife of Abraham Lincoln

Robert Lincoln
the Lincolns' oldest son

Tad (Thomas) Lincoln
the Lincolns' youngest son

Willie (William) Lincoln
the Lincolns' middle son

James Luckett
Baltimore businessman and friend of Ferrandini

Allan Pinkerton
America's most famous lawman and founder of
the Pinkerton National Detective Agency

Winfield Scott
commanding general of the U.S. Army and official
in charge of security in Washington, D.C.

Frederick Seward
journalist and son of Senator William H. Seward

William H. Seward
U.S. senator from New York and Lincoln's secretary of state

Charles Stone
U.S. army officer and assistant to General Winfield Scott

Kate Warne
agent of the Pinkerton National Detective Agency and
America's first professional woman detective

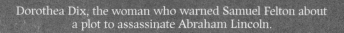
Dorothea Dix, the woman who warned Samuel Felton about
a plot to assassinate Abraham Lincoln.

Prologue

THE WARNING

Philadelphia, Pennsylvania
January 1861

On a cold winter's day, a tall woman with delicate features strode into the Philadelphia office of Mr. Samuel Felton. And Felton—the president of the Philadelphia, Wilmington, and Baltimore Railroad—wondered why his distinguished visitor had come.

In her tidy, respectable bonnet and hoop skirt, she might have passed for any ordinary housewife. But Miss Dorothea Dix was not ordinary. She was a strong, determined human rights advocate who had won fame by forcing officials to provide decent, humane care for prisoners and the mentally ill. But on this particular January day, the well-known activist was not in the office to discuss the rights of convicts or patients.

She had come to talk about . . . danger.

During a recent trip to Kentucky, Miss Dix had learned that a band of slavery-loving southerners had decided to prevent Abraham Lincoln—a well-known opponent of slavery—from being sworn in as president of the United States.

To do this, the group was secretly plotting to overthrow the national government, seize the nation's capital, and then blow up Felton's railroad as well as all other railways that connected the slave-free North to Washington, D.C., and the slave-owning states of the South.

No. Miss Dix didn't know the names of the conspirators, but it seemed likely that the strike would come while Lincoln was traveling from his home in Springfield, Illinois, to the nation's capital. And that meant these fanatics might try to blow up the president-elect's train while he was riding through the southern slave state of Maryland—on Mr. Felton's railway line.

Shaken, Felton struggled to digest the news. What he'd just heard was shocking. It was dreadful. But . . . was it true? Was there really a plot to overthrow the government, destroy his railroad, and kill the new president? And, if there was, what could an ordinary businessman like Samuel Felton do about it?

He couldn't report the problem to the FBI. In 1861, there was no Federal Bureau of Investigation. There was no Central Intelligence Agency. There was no Secret Service or national government police of any kind.

Could he warn President-Elect Lincoln? Maybe. But how? There were no telephones, and a letter might take weeks to arrive. In 1861, only the telegraph could relay an instantaneous message. But telegrams were not secret. They were sent and received by operators, and a dishonest operator might start a panic by leaking information about the plot to the newspapers.

But if Felton ignored the warning . . . if he sat still . . . if he did nothing, these southern hotheads might destroy the government or kill Mr. Lincoln. And the death of this newly elected president, this president who believed that slavery must eventually end in all parts of America, might well change U.S. history.

To Samuel Felton, the responsibility was clear. Somehow, he had to find out the facts. He had to protect the nation, his railroad, and Mr. Lincoln.

But how on earth was he going to do it?

An early campaign portrait of Abraham Lincoln,
the Republican presidential candidate.

Chapter 1

"WHAT DOES ANYONE WANT TO HARM ME FOR?"

Springfield, Illinois
January 1861

Abraham Lincoln, however, didn't think he needed protection.

Half a continent away from Philadelphia, he was sprawled on an old sofa in his cluttered Illinois law office. He hadn't heard Miss Dix's news. He wasn't stewing about plots. But he had plenty of other things to think about.

After all, just two months ago—on November 7,

1860—he'd been elected president of the United States.

Yes, it had been just about two months since he'd burst through the front door of his house and told his excited wife, "Mary, *we* are elected." It had been barely sixty days since that amazing election night when, unable to sleep, he'd suddenly felt the great weight of presidential "responsibility that was upon [him]." Now, in just a few more weeks—on February 11—he'd be leaving his old home in Springfield, Illinois, and heading to Washington, D.C. Then, on March 4, he would be inaugurated— officially sworn in—as the sixteenth president of the United States.

But, although his new job hadn't really started, in some ways Abraham Lincoln was "sick of office-holding" already. Ever since election night he'd been bombarded with letters, questions, and problems. He'd been pestered by hundreds of people who wanted government jobs. For several days he'd had to do his own housekeeping because Mrs. Lincoln was off in New York City buying a bunch of fancy first lady dresses. He had to rent out his house, sell some furniture, try on his inaugural suit, pack up his belongings, and make a million decisions. There were decisions about who to appoint to his cabinet, decisions about what to do or say in public. Goodness, because a little girl had written to say that he'd look better with whiskers, he'd even decided to grow a beard.

And that was the small stuff. The big decision—the one that weighed on Abraham Lincoln like a hundred-thousand-pound gorilla—was: How was he going to fix America? How was he going to fix a country that had just broken into two separate parts—because Americans couldn't agree about slavery?

Of course, this fight about slavery wasn't new. Abraham Lincoln was all too well aware of that. Just like almost every other person in the country, he knew that Americans had been arguing about whether slavery was bad or good ever since 1619, when the first twenty African slaves had been sold in Virginia.

During that time, most northerners had decided that slavery was evil. They believed it had no place in a country whose Declaration of Independence said that all "are created equal" and that each has a right to "Life, Liberty, and the pursuit of Happiness." So in the North—where thousands of immigrants were willing to do hard work for low pay, and most people made money by manufacturing goods or providing business services—slaves and slavery had gradually disappeared.

But in the South, things were different. There, where many grew tobacco or cotton for a living, white southerners had found that it was easy and cheap to have Black slaves tend those important, moneymaking crops. Since farmers needed lots of workers, the number of slaves in the South had gradually increased to about four million. White southerners came to believe that having slaves was a "Positive Good," and they soon wanted to spread slavery into all the new states in the American West. But doing that wasn't easy, because when white southerners tried to bring Black slaves into the new western states and territories, northerners objected.

And the argument about slavery suddenly exploded. All over America people began to quarrel furiously about whether each new state should be a slave state (a state where slavery was legal under state law) or a free state (where state law made it illegal to keep slaves). And they didn't just yell and shake their fists. Instead, they rioted, they burned barns, and sometimes they beat up enemies or shot opponents with guns. In one part of Kansas, an army of several hundred slavery supporters looted a town and burned the houses and shops of those who wanted Kansas to be a free state. But in another part of Kansas territory, abolitionists (people who wanted slavery to be abolished—banned—immediately) attacked pro-slavery men with swords. And the violence even spread to Washington, D.C. There, in the nation's Capitol Building, Preston Brooks, a congressman from the slave state of South Carolina, used his cane to wallop Massachusetts senator Charles Sumner into a bloody pulp.

Why? Because the Massachusetts man said that trying

to make slavery legal in Kansas was a crime against God.

Each year there was more trouble. More violence. Then, in 1860—just when it seemed the fight couldn't get much worse—Abraham Lincoln ran for president.

And Abraham Lincoln hated slavery. To him, it was a "monstrous injustice" that was destroying the free soul of America. It was, he said, "the evil out of which all other national evils and dangers have come." "If slavery is not wrong," Lincoln told people, "nothing is wrong."

But in 1860, the U.S. Constitution—the basic set of laws that governed the entire nation—still allowed all American citizens to legally own slaves. White southerners, of course, didn't want to give up their valuable Black workers. So, in the hopes of uniting the country, Abraham Lincoln offered voters a compromise: Let slavery continue in the fifteen states where it already existed, but make slavery illegal in any new states or territories that might be added to the federal Union. Free states, he figured, would soon outnumber slave states, and, over time, slavery would gradually disappear.

Although abolitionists objected, most northerners thought this plan sounded pretty reasonable. Southerners, however, absolutely hated the idea. And, most of all, they hated that "ill-bred, profane, vulgar" devil of a "jackass"—Abraham Lincoln.

They hated Lincoln so much that on Election Day

almost no one in the slave-holding South voted for him.

But Lincoln won anyway.

And that angered southerners. It made them so red-hot, rip-roaring mad that forty-three days after Abraham Lincoln was elected, the slave state of South Carolina seceded. It backed out of the federal Union and decided to leave the United States for good—just because the state's citizens hated the idea of having a president who'd said that the United States could not continue to be "half-*slave* and half-*free*."

And that was only the beginning.

By February 1, six other slave states—Mississippi, Florida, Alabama, Georgia, Louisiana, and Texas—had also left the Union.

Soon the runaway states formed their own country: the Confederate States of America. Then, on February 9, they chose a former U.S. senator named Jefferson Davis to be their very own president.

Suddenly there were two Americas—and two presidents. The nation was broken. And what was Mr. Lincoln going to do about it?

Would he let the runaway southern states take their slaves and go in peace? Would he fight a war to bring them back into the Union, or would he give in? Would he let southerners bring their slaves into some new states just to reunite the nation? No one knew. And Mr. Lincoln? Well, he wasn't saying.

When newspaper reporters asked about secession, he made vague statements. "Let us . . . remember," he'd say, "that all American citizens are brothers of a common country." He let the public think he had no opinions and no policy.

But that wasn't true—because Abraham Lincoln did have very definite ideas about the national crisis.

Alone, in a dusty locked room on the third floor of his brother-in-law's store, he'd set down those ideas in his inauguration speech. For days he'd worked on that speech. He'd jotted down ideas on little pieces of paper. He'd written and rewritten drafts in pencil. And, while he was writing, he'd kept that speech secret. Top secret. Finally, to keep it safe from prying eyes, he'd locked the finished manuscript in a little black satchel that he planned to take with him to Washington. And if Mr. Lincoln had his way, no member of the general public would know what his speech said until Inauguration Day.

As long as no one knew what he'd written, there was no chance that his words could make another state secede or start a civil war. And that was important. It was important because if other states seceded or if someone fired a shot, big decisions would have to be made about war and peace. And Lincoln would not have the power to make those decisions until after he had been legally sworn in as president on Inauguration Day.

So, for the moment, Mr. Lincoln said little. He kept his thoughts to himself. He let people wonder whether he favored compromise or confrontation. And he knew that everyone would find out the answer when he gave his inauguration speech.

If he lived long enough to deliver it.

Ever since Election Day, death threats had been pouring into the Lincoln mailbox. One southerner threatened to shoot the new president on March 4. Another sent a horrible picture of Lincoln with a hangman's noose around his neck, "his feet chained and his body adorned with tar and feathers." Some of the mail was so vicious that friends thought Lincoln should wear armor and have his food tasted for poison. "They'll kill ye, Abe," the president's old friend Hannah Armstrong told him. And Lincoln's stepmother was so afraid that "something would happen" to her "Abe" that she'd begged him not to run for president. But, of course, Lincoln had run. He'd been elected, and he'd also burned bushels of those ugly letters. Over and over, he'd said that the danger was "all imagination." He'd even comforted his stepmother by telling her to, "Trust in the Lord, and all will be well." And that was all perfectly fine—except for the little secret something Mr. Lincoln didn't tell those worried folks. He didn't tell them that he had already seen a sign of his own death.

One day soon after the election, he'd looked in the mirror and seen himself with two faces. One looked pink and healthy. But the other was deadly pale. What did it mean? he'd asked his wife. That you'll be elected twice, but not live out your second term, she'd said.

And maybe that was right. Maybe death would come in five years, six years, or seven. But maybe it would come in days or weeks. Maybe it would come tomorrow. . . .

Still, Lincoln was a practical man. He was a lawyer who believed in hard evidence and "unimpassioned reason." He wasn't scared by spooks. And he had no time to brood about an eerie vision. So when people talked to him about death threats, Mr. Lincoln shrugged and said, "What does anyone want to harm me for?" After all, he pointed out, there was no need for violence. He'd only been elected for one four-year term. After that, he said, "I can be turned out, and a better man with better views put in my place."

Besides, killing one man wouldn't solve the nation's problems. And surely Americans wouldn't kill a president just because they disagreed with him. . . .

Would they?

HOME OF ABRAHAM LINCOLN.
Springfield, Ill. 1860.
He left it in peace, to preside over a nation, then in bondage.
He now reposes under its soil a martyr to the Freedom he won.

The home Abraham Lincoln lived in until he
left Springfield, Illinois, to become president.

Chapter 2

MR. PINKERTON TAKES THE CASE

Philadelphia, Pennsylvania
January 1861

But would they? Would a gang of angry southerners really try to seize the capital, overthrow the government, and kill the president-elect? For days those questions had been whirling through Samuel Felton's mind. For days the anxious railroad executive had waited for proof that what Miss Dix had said was true. And now, at last, he had some news.

Though the spies he'd sent south hadn't uncovered any new information about a specific plot to murder Lincoln, their reports were still disturbing. During their investigations, these agents had heard additional rumors that southern hotheads wanted to cut ties between Washington, D.C., and the northern states by blowing up all the railroad bridges and ferries in the state of Maryland. And that possibility was scary. It was scary because Felton's trains had to use those bridges and ferries. But it wasn't the chance of railway damage or disruption that was really alarming. It was the fact that the only way Mr. Lincoln could reach Washington was by traveling through Maryland on Felton's railroad. And if some fanatic blew up a railroad bridge while Lincoln's train was crossing, the explosion might kill the new president.

The danger was clear, and now Felton had to act. To prevent disaster, he had to find out who might be planning these attacks. He needed to know when and where these enemies might strike. And he needed to know fast. It was now late in January. On February 11, Lincoln would be leaving his Illinois home, and on February 23 he was scheduled to travel through Maryland on Felton's line. That left barely a month, a scant thirty or so days, to find the plotters and thwart their plans. It was a tall order. And Felton knew there was only one man in the whole United States who could possibly fill it.

Swiftly, the railroad executive picked up his pen and addressed a letter to Mr. Allan Pinkerton, the founder of the Pinkerton National Detective Agency, America's only major, first-class, nation-wide security service. Would Mr. Pinkerton please come to Philadelphia immediately, Felton wrote, to discuss "a matter of great importance"?

At his Chicago headquarters Allan Pinkerton read the letter, sized up the situation, and got ready to move. After asking his assistants to take care of the agency's current crop of railroad security, counterfeiting, and mail-theft cases, the detective quickly packed a bag and headed for the railway station. Soon he was speeding toward Philadelphia, and in no time the head of the Pinkerton National Detective Agency was shaking hands with Samuel Felton, president of the Philadelphia, Wilmington, and Baltimore Railroad.

As America's number one lawman entered the railroad office, Felton must have looked at him curiously. In person the country's most famous detective was a chunky, middle-size, muscular man with rust-colored hair. Pinkerton's features were average, ordinary, and forgettable. But his penetrating blue-gray eyes missed nothing, and he listened intently as Felton presented the facts.

Once the problem was clear, the two men devised a plan. Felton would station about two hundred reliable men to guard the bridges and ferries along the most vulnerable thirty-seven-mile stretch of his railway line. By day, these guards would pretend to be painters and carpenters assigned to repair the railroad bridges and boats. At night, they would be on the lookout for trouble.

Pinkerton himself would take on the challenge of ferreting out the names of the conspirators and discovering the details of the plot.

To do so, he would station undercover agents in various towns along the railroad route that seemed to be particular centers of unrest. Each targeted town would be a place where the citizens were fanatically pro-slavery, where support for the new secessionist movement was high, and where residents voiced a passionate hatred of Abraham Lincoln. The spies, of course, would be Pinkerton's best agents. They would be smart, reliable, tough, alert, and willing to work around the clock. Each man and woman would constantly bear in mind that the Pinkerton trademark was a wide-awake, all-seeing eye and that the agency's motto was "We Never Sleep."

For himself, the detective reserved the difficult job of simultaneously acting as an undercover agent and running his spy network. It would be a big undertaking. And it would be dangerous—because Maryland was a very unfriendly place.

A large number of state residents wanted Maryland to secede from the Union and join the Confederacy. Even the state governor had declared that he personally didn't want to live without slavery. Only 2.5 percent of all Maryland voters had cast their ballots for Lincoln, and the new president was so unpopular that six men who'd dared to vote for him were kicked out of one Maryland county.

As he left Samuel Felton's office and stepped out into the winter chill, Allan Pinkerton knew he had his work cut out for him. But Pinkerton, a self-made man who'd started life as a poor, hungry boy in a Scottish slum, had never shied away from danger or difficulty. First as a deputy sheriff and later as a private eye, he'd taken on some of the country's worst criminals. He'd tangled with bank robbers, train robbers, and murderers. But this time the fate of the country and the life of its new president were riding squarely on his shoulders. It was the greatest challenge he'd ever faced. And for Pinkerton, this mission was not just another professional commission. It was part of his own personal crusade to end slavery.

As a dedicated abolitionist and a longtime conductor on the Underground Railroad, Pinkerton had done everything he could to help free American slaves. For him, it was personally important to make sure that southern pro-slavery secessionists didn't take over the country. And it was personally important to ensure that Abraham Lincoln, a man who called slavery a "vast moral evil," was sworn in as president.

Now, as he walked down the Philadelphia streets,

Pinkerton knew that his mission was difficult. His time was short. His responsibility was great. And the stakes for the country were enormous.

Although he never admitted it, Allan Pinkerton must have been just a little nervous.

Portrait of Allan Pinkerton showing the detective's legendary keen-eyed gaze.

Chapter 3

A VISIT TO MOBTOWN

Maryland
Late January-February 10, 1861

The wheels clanked. The whistle blew. Allan Pinkerton looked out the train window, but he wasn't interested in the scenery. As his train made its way south through the slave state of Maryland, the detective searched for places to station his spies.

At Havre de Grace the steamboats carrying Felton's railway cars from the Pennsylvania side of the Susquehanna River to the Maryland side were an obvious target. So Pinkerton left one man there to look for suspicious activity.

In Perrymansville, the detective heard furious

secessionist citizens swearing that "no d—d abolitionist should be allowed to pass through the town alive." It was definitely a hotspot, and Pinkerton decided to station Agent Timothy Webster in the village. When Webster asked for orders, the detective told his "daring," dark-haired young spy to mingle with the population, pretend to be a southern sympathizer, and watch out for anyone who "attempted violence" or showed a "disposition to resort to aggressive measures."

On through Maryland Pinkerton went. He checked out towns, he instructed agents, and finally he reached Baltimore.

Some people called Maryland's biggest city Mobtown, and the name fit. Baltimore was a tough, violent place with a long history of trouble. Forty-nine years earlier, a band of Baltimore thugs had attacked Revolutionary War hero "Light Horse" Harry Lee. They'd beaten him senseless, hurled him down a flight of stairs, and almost cut off his nose—simply because Lee had dared to support a newspaper that opposed the War of 1812. Then, in 1857, there was another incident. This time a mob protested the election of U.S. president James Buchanan by pelting the nation's new chief executive with stones and bricks. Armed gangs like the Plug Uglies, the Rough Skins, the Black Snakes, and the Blood Tubs (who ducked their enemies in pails of pigs' blood) ruled the streets. They terrorized the residents, and they turned Baltimore into a murder capital. Even going to the polls to vote was dangerous because gangs often beat up citizens who didn't support the mobsters' favorite candidates. Since different gangs supported different political parties, huge mobs sometimes battled one another at election time with axes, bricks, picks, and guns until "the gutters flowed with rivers of blood."

In 1861, however, the city was more than just a fountain of violence; it was also a thriving center of the slave trade.

Although more free black people lived in Baltimore than in most other places in America, many of its white citizens made their money by buying, selling, and transporting thousands of enslaved African Americans. People who walked down Baltimore's Pratt Street passed a slave prison where chained Black men were penned with Black women, children, and babies in a bare brick yard open to the scorching sun and pouring rain. White attacks on African Americans were common, and the famous Black abolitionist and former slave Frederick Douglass remembered that he'd once been so badly "cut and bruised" by Baltimore thugs that his left eye was "nearly knocked out of its socket."

In Baltimore slavery and secession were popular, and the new U.S. president was so thoroughly hated that

Lincoln's few Baltimore supporters were attacked with bricks, eggs, and curses when they celebrated Lincoln's nomination for president by parading through town.

As Pinkerton wandered through the city, talking to locals, listening to conversations, and assessing the political situation, he smelled trouble. The mood in the city was ugly. No abolitionist, Yankee, or Union supporter was safe on a Baltimore street. The city felt like a spot where murder plots could breed like toadstools. It was ripe for investigation, and the detective knew it was the perfect spot for his headquarters.

Calling himself John H. Hutcheson and pretending to be a southern secessionist stockbroker, Pinkerton rented an office at 44 South Street. The place was conveniently located near the stations of Baltimore's three railroads, and the building had four entrances—one on each side—making it easy for agents to come and go secretly.

Once he had prepared the South Street center of operations, the detective got on with his next job: stationing some of his best agents around the city.

First, Pinkerton took care of Harry Davies, a gifted investigator who spoke several languages, had once trained as a Jesuit priest, and had lived in New Orleans for several years. Davies was suave. He sounded like a resident of the South. And since he had the manners of an aristocrat, he was the perfect person to spy on Baltimore's high-society secessionists. After filling the agent's pockets with money, Pinkerton told Davies to rent a room in one of Baltimore's most expensive hotels, pose as a rich southerner, and pretend that he would do anything to promote southern rights and prevent the inauguration of Abraham Lincoln.

To Agent Kate Warne, America's first professional woman detective, Pinkerton gave an entirely different assignment. This slender, brown-haired, blue-eyed twenty-eight-year-old was a brave, vivacious, clever conversationalist who could get information out of almost any man or woman. Allan Pinkerton had originally hired her in 1856 because she said she could "worm out secrets in many places to which it was impossible for male detectives to gain access." In five years of work, young Mrs. Warne had never disappointed him. But both she and Pinkerton knew her new job would be tricky. Acting the part of a southern belle and wearing the black-and-white ribbon rosette of a secession supporter pinned to her dress, Mrs. Warne was to rent a room in a Baltimore boardinghouse. There, she was to sit, sew, and gossip with the residents in order to find out if their friends or relatives were involved in anti-Lincoln, secessionist activities.

With that settled, Pinkerton started to investigate on his own, and, almost immediately, the detective stumbled on a possible lead.

Soon after moving into the South Street building, he

met a fellow tenant named James Luckett. At first the two men just said a casual how-do-you-do, and Pinkerton introduced himself as John H. Hutcheson, a stockbroker from Georgia. Soon, however, the conversation turned to politics. When Pinkerton pretended to be a passionate supporter of southern rights, Luckett revealed that he was praying for Maryland to secede. He was desperate to see southern troops take over Washington, and, of course, he hated Lincoln. But had Luckett heard of any conspiracies? Was he personally involved in a plot? Pinkerton must have been dying to ask. But before the detective could pose those sensitive, leading questions, he had to earn Luckett's trust. That, of course, would take time. It would take persistence. And it might not pan out. So while he was waiting and hoping to find out more from Luckett, Pinkerton searched for other leads.

At night the detective took himself to Barnum's Hotel, where a large group of the city's slavery-loving, secessionist fire-eaters regularly gathered for drinks and conversation. As the talk swirled around, Pinkerton was alarmed. The hotel was jammed with angry armed southerners who damned Lincoln, longed for Maryland's secession, and feverishly swore that they would give their lives to defend slavery and southern rights.

But were these men big talkers or real terrorists?

Were any of them really angry enough to blow up a train?

Were they crazy enough to murder a president?

Pinkerton suspected that some of them were. But which?

Which of these men should he follow? Whom should he investigate? With time and patience, he could find out—but the clock was ticking. The date on the calendar was now February 10. In just twenty-four hours, on February 11, 1861, Abraham Lincoln would leave Springfield, Illinois, and begin his trip to Washington. The president-elect was scheduled to arrive in Baltimore on February 23. So Pinkerton had just twelve days to uncover a possible plot. Twelve days to ensure the new president's safety. Twelve days to crack the case.

And at the moment he didn't have a single solid clue.

Abraham Lincoln's oldest son, Robert, who carried
the satchel containing his father's inaugural address.

Chapter 4

"I BID YOU AN AFFECTIONATE FAREWELL."

Springfield, Illinois
February 11, 1861

There was no question about it. President-Elect Abraham Lincoln was not a happy man.

In just a little while he had to board the train that would take him on the first leg of his journey to Washington. He'd packed his bags. He'd addressed his parcels to "A. Lincoln, White House, Washington, D.C." He'd handed the little black satchel containing his precious, top secret inaugural address to his seventeen-year-old son, Robert, and warned the youngster not to lose the bag or let it out of his sight.

Everything had seemed fine when the brand-new

president got out of bed that morning. But now, minutes before he had to leave for the station to catch the eight a.m. train, his wife, Mary, was lying on the floor crying because Mr. Lincoln had refused to give a government job to one of her friends.

It wasn't that Abraham Lincoln didn't love his wife, and it wasn't that his wife didn't love him. They cared for each other so deeply that Mary Lincoln always spoke of her "sainted" or "idolized" husband. Even at the start of their marriage, when many had laughed at Lincoln's lack of schooling and backwoods manners, she'd believed that one day her husband would be president of the United States.

Abraham Lincoln, on the other hand, had been so entranced by witty, pretty, shrewd Mary that he'd had her wedding ring engraved with the heartfelt words "Love is eternal." But, in addition to being smart and attractive, Mary Todd Lincoln was a high-strung woman who liked getting her own way. And she was trying to do that now.

Still, in their eighteen years of marriage, the Lincolns had had other disagreements. Each time they'd made up. And—although neither ever explained exactly how—they made up this time too. Mary Lincoln dried her tears. She tidied her hair, put on her bonnet, and joined her husband and sons on the horse-drawn bus that would take them to the Springfield railroad station.

Outside, the weather was cold, damp, and gloomy, but despite heavy rain clouds, a huge crowd had gathered at the station. Almost a thousand people—most of whom Lincoln recognized—had come to see him off. At the sight of so many longtime friends and neighbors, the new president's face turned "pale" and "quivered with emotion." Parting was hard, and as he made his way toward the platform, clasping hundreds of outstretched hands, the president-elect seemed so overcome by his feelings that he could barely speak.

Fat raindrops splashed down. Some opened umbrellas. But Lincoln didn't seem to care about the weather. Briefly, he turned to say goodbye to his family. Although young Robert would be traveling with his father today, Mrs. Lincoln and her two other sons, ten-year-old Willie and seven-year-old Tad, would be leaving later to join the president-elect in Indianapolis the next day.

But now the engineer was waiting. Clock hands were inching past eight, and it was time for the final farewell. Slowly, Abraham Lincoln shook a few last hands, climbed aboard, and turned to the waiting crowd. For a moment he stood—a tall, thin, gangly figure in a black suit silhouetted against the yellow painted train cars. Then, as the crowd waited, he took off his hat and began to speak.

"My friends," he said. "No one, not in my situation, can appreciate my feeling of sadness at this parting. To this place, and the kindness of these people, I owe everything. Here I have lived a quarter of a century, and have passed from [being] a young to an old man. . . . I now leave, not knowing when, or whether ever, I may return, with a task before me greater than that which rested upon [the first president of the United States, George] Washington. Without the assistance of [God] . . . I cannot succeed. With that assistance I cannot fail. . . . [So] . . . let us confidently hope that all will yet be well. To His care . . . I hope in your prayers you will commend me. I bid you an affectionate farewell."

Some shouted out, "We will pray for you." Others cheered. And as the train pulled away, Mr. Lincoln remained standing at the rear doorway of his car, a single lonesome figure, looking back at Springfield.

Inside the train, Lincoln's son Robert and the president-elect's traveling team of about twenty secretaries, advisors, and friends waited. But Abraham Lincoln didn't seem to want to talk to any of them. Instead, he sat alone, silent and withdrawn. But whether he was brooding about the sadness of his departure, the tremendous responsibilities that awaited him in Washington, or the long journey ahead of him, no one knew.

At a time when there were no TVs, no radios, no computers, and no photographs in newspapers, Mr. Lincoln felt it was important to give the American people a chance to see him in person. So his advisors had arranged a two-thousand-mile, twelve-day trip that would take the new president across the country to Washington. On the way he would travel through seven states, ride on eighteen different railroads, and make seventy-five planned stops at cities and towns along the route.

To make sure that all Americans knew exactly where they could see and hear the new president, newspapers had published his schedule in detail. In edition after edition they had printed the date of his visit to each city, the times of his arrival and departure, the locations of the railway stations he'd use, and the names of the hotels he'd stay in. For the next twelve days, every newspaper reader in the country would know exactly where to find the president-elect at any hour of the day or night. All Mr. Lincoln's friends, admirers, and supporters would be able to locate him instantly. But all of Mr. Lincoln's enemies would be able to find him as well.

And enemies were a potential problem—because no one on the Lincoln team had made any serious plans to protect the president-elect.

Despite the bushels of death threats Abraham Lincoln had received since his election, the new president had no real security escort. No formal plans had been made by his staff to have extra police on hand to safeguard Lincoln during his visits to towns and cities. No watchmen had been stationed along railway lines to make sure his train wasn't ambushed, and—although Lincoln was accompanied by several able-bodied military advisors and friends—there were absolutely no professional bodyguards aboard the president-elect's train.

Still, in the 1800s, people didn't worry about a president's safety as much as we do today. In those days, U.S. presidents weren't usually accompanied by special police escorts. No one then thought that a U.S. president needed any kind of special protection, and none of Mr. Lincoln's advisors believed there was any particular reason to fear an attack. The president-elect, after all, would mostly be traveling through the northern free states, where he was quite popular. And Mr. Lincoln himself had said time and time again that he didn't believe there was any real danger. Since the new president wasn't the kind of man who hated political enemies or wanted to harm them, he found it hard to believe that political foes could hate or want to harm him. The best way to deal with opponents, he said cheerfully, was to "do good to those who hate you and turn their ill will into friendship."

Still, Lincoln and his advisors weren't fools. They did know that some citizens violently disagreed with the president-elect. They certainly must have figured that Mr. Lincoln would meet a few rowdy protesters along the way. But no one expected serious trouble. So, as their train chugged across the prairies, the new president's advisors talked about politics and discussed their trip. None of them suspected that a group of southern fanatics might be making plans to murder Abraham Lincoln. And none of them guessed that the president-elect might actually be in danger.

Jefferson Davis, a former U.S. senator from Mississippi who became president of the Confederate States of America.

Chapter 5

"BOTH SEXES AND ALL AGES ARE FOR WAR."

Illinois, Mississippi, Maryland
February 11, 1861

Danger, however, was in the air, and many Americans knew it. The year had scarcely begun, but already some were calling 1861 a disaster. Seven states had left the Union. The country had broken apart. Newspapers were talking about a civil war between North and South. And on February 11, there was another alarming sign. As anxious citizens drank their morning coffee, many realized that for the first time ever, *two different American presidents* were about to take office.

In Springfield, Illinois, Abraham Lincoln, the new U.S. president, was saying farewell to his hometown, boarding a train, and setting out to celebrate his March 4 inauguration in Washington, D.C.

And in Mississippi, at almost the very same moment, Jefferson Davis, the recently chosen president of the seceded southern states, was also on his way to his own presidential swearing-in ceremony.

After saying goodbye to his wife, the new president of the Confederate States of America left his eight-hundred-acre cotton plantation. He climbed into a small boat and ordered a group of slaves to row him three miles down the river. There, Davis boarded the *Natchez*, a regularly scheduled steamboat. It would take him to Vicksburg, Mississippi—the first stop on a five-day journey to his February 18 inauguration in Montgomery, Alabama.

Tall and thin with a gaunt, hawklike face and a rigid personality, Davis had not really wanted to become president of the new Confederacy. As a West Point graduate and experienced military man, he'd wanted to lead the southern army. But when selected by delegates at a Confederate convention, the former U.S. senator and U.S. secretary of war had felt duty-bound to accept his new nation's number one job.

Still, although Jefferson Davis wasn't sure he'd make a good president, most other white southerners thought he was the perfect man for the job. And no wonder.

Like most white southerners, Davis passionately believed in slavery.

Like most white southerners, he passionately believed in secession.

And, like many of his fellow white southerners, he believed that a civil war between the South and the North was the only way to permanently settle the great American dispute over slavery. To keep their slaves and defend their way of life, white southerners were willing to fight, and war fever was raging through the southern states.

"Both sexes and all ages are for war. . . ." one journalist reported. "Young ladies sing for it; old ladies pray for it; young men are dying for it; old men are ready to demonstrate it."

So, naturally, the Vicksburg crowds cheered when Jefferson Davis said he was willing to shed "every drop of my blood" for the twin causes of slavery and secession.

And most white southerners were wildly enthusiastic when President-Elect Davis predicted that "there would be war, long and bloody."

But not every southerner thought the answer was all-out war.

In Baltimore, Maryland, a small group of men were

considering another solution. Since these people believed that the election of Abraham Lincoln had caused all the nation's problems, they felt that the best way to resolve America's difficulties was to kill the new president.

In shadowy Baltimore rooms, a group of fanatic southerners began to talk of murder. Some whispered about guns and knives while others probably spoke of bombs. Together they secretly began to plan the death of Mr. Lincoln. And as the new U.S. president was traveling toward Washington, these would-be assassins were deciding how, when, and where to kill him.

Chapter 6

GONE!

Indianapolis, Indiana
February 11, 1861

Flags were flying, crowds were cheering, and people were waving when the *Lincoln Special* pulled into the Indianapolis station promptly at five p.m.

After shaking the governor's hand and listening to soldiers fire a thirty-four-gun salute (one gun for each state), the new U.S. president climbed into an open carriage drawn by four white horses and paraded through the red-white-and-blue-decked Indianapolis streets.

It looked like the whole city had turned out to see Mr. Lincoln. The crowds were thick. The cheers were loud, and so many well-wishers were waiting at his hotel that the president-elect could barely squeeze through the door. Inside, the fancy Bates House was filled to bursting. A mass of people was packed tight in the lobby. Men and women blocked the stairs. Almost three thousand people were waiting to shake the new president's hand, and—while Mr. Lincoln shook and shook until his own fingers were puffy and painful—another crowd of twenty thousand stood outside calling for a speech.

But what was Lincoln going to say?

For weeks he'd refused to talk about his plans for dealing with America's problems. For fear of making matters worse before he was sworn in as president, Mr. Lincoln had kept his thoughts about the national crisis to himself. He'd decided that no one was going to know exactly what his views were on war, peace, or secession until he delivered his top secret inaugural speech on March 4. But now he was stuck. Within minutes he had to stand on the hotel balcony and make a speech to twenty thousand people—who all wanted to know how he was going to fix the country.

So what on earth was he going to say?

The answer was: nothing. And no one was better at saying nothing than the new president.

Once, when he didn't want to reveal what he really thought about a book, Abraham Lincoln said, "For those who like this sort of thing, this is exactly the sort of thing they would like."

But talking about the fate of America was a lot trickier than talking about a book. In this tense situation, even one awkward phrase could start a war or make another state secede.

So, as he stepped out on the hotel balcony and faced the crowd, Mr. Lincoln started with the easy stuff. He thanked the citizens of Indianapolis for their "magnificent welcome" and their "generous support." But at this moment, the president-elect explained, he didn't think it was wise to discuss the current national situation. When folks were quarreling—the way the North and South were now—he said, it was better to "keep silence" than to jump into the argument. Still, Mr. Lincoln said, there was an important question that people might want to think about. If, he said, the federal Union was like a marriage, did states have the right to get out of that marriage whenever they felt like it? Now, he wasn't offering an answer. He was just asking a question. He was only asking people to consider. He was only asking them to think.

Then, before anyone in the crowd had time to consider, think, or realize that the new president hadn't really told them anything, Mr. Lincoln said goodbye and darted back inside his hotel.

It was late now, and time for a meal.

But, apparently, no one had given much thought to supper.

Although Mr. Lincoln and a few of his advisors had planned to have a quiet dinner together, no one had ordered the food or arranged for a private dining room. So now the only place for the new president to eat was in the overcrowded hotel restaurant where plates were crashing, food was flying, and guests were shouting for service. As distracted, overworked waiters raced between tables, one man had sugar spilled over his back. Another ordered tea and got a sour pickle. And the whole situation was so ridiculous that Mr. Lincoln just burst out laughing.

Somehow, though, the president-elect's party managed to swallow a few bites. The crowd began to clear, and finally Mr. Lincoln went up to his room to relax. Inside, his bed was waiting. His clothes were there. Everything was fine . . . except that the little black satchel containing his top secret inaugural address didn't seem to be in his bedroom.

It wasn't behind the door—or sitting on a chair. It wasn't under the bed. No. The thing was missing. It was gone. Just plain *gone*.

But where?

Only that morning Mr. Lincoln had handed the satchel to his son. He'd told Robert to hold on to that bag for dear life. He'd warned the teenager not to let the thing out of his sight. And now both the bag and the speech inside had vanished. In a panic, the president-elect called his son.

Where, Mr. Lincoln wanted to know, was the little black oilcloth satchel?

The satchel? Oh, said Robert, he'd given it to a hotel employee. To a waiter. Or a porter. Someone like that.

And where had this waiter or porter put it?

Well, maybe in the baggage room . . .

Now, Abraham Lincoln was a very patient, loving father. Since he believed that children should be "free, happy, and unrestrained by parental tyranny," he never yelled. He didn't scold his children for playing with his treasured books. He never got mad when they spilled his ink or messed with important papers. But this was too much.

Mr. Lincoln exploded. He chewed Robert out. Then he raced downstairs to find his bag.

In the hotel baggage room, he began digging through piles of luggage. He threw suitcases here and boxes there. He opened a black oilcloth satchel that looked like his. But the only things inside were a dirty shirt and a bottle of whisky. Frantic, the president-elect kept looking. Then he saw it. A locked black bag. His key fitted. And . . . yes . . . inside there was a wad of papers. It was his inaugural address. No one had tampered with it. No one had given it to the newspapers. His secret speech was safe—and his true opinions about war, peace, and the secession crisis were still secret.

But it had been an awfully near thing, and Mr. Lincoln had learned an important lesson. From now on he would keep an eye on that satchel himself. He would carry it with his own hands. And he would make sure that it stayed safe.

But, at the moment, it was late. Tomorrow the president-elect's wife and two younger boys would be arriving early. Then the whole family had to catch the ten thirty a.m. train to Cincinnati for another marathon of crowds and speeches. It would be another long day, and all the members of the Lincoln team were probably glad to get to their beds.

Still, for everyone in the president's party, February 11 had been an amazing experience. The crowds, the cheers, and the wild enthusiasm had been wonderful and exhilarating. But those dense, crazy, shoving masses of people had been scary, too.

As he thought back over the day, one of Lincoln's secretaries, John Nicolay, realized that there had been times when the vast, frenzied, thrusting, jostling crowds could have accidentally "killed" or hurt his boss. And if this friendly Indianapolis crowd had almost injured the president-elect, it was clear that a violent, angry, hostile crowd could easily murder him.

Back in Springfield, the job of protecting the new president had seemed pretty simple and unimportant. Then, nobody on the Lincoln team had thought that taking the president-elect through a lot of crowds on this cross-country trip posed any serious danger.

But now, a worried Nicolay was not so sure.

Artwork depicting the Lincoln family. Abraham Lincoln
was an affectionate father who loved spending time with his children.

Chapter 7

"I WOULD LIKE TO TELL YOU, BUT I DARE NOT."

Baltimore, Maryland
February 10-12, 1861

Danger. Danger. Danger. There was no way that Allan Pinkerton could stop thinking about it. Each day the time of Lincoln's visit to Baltimore came closer. Each day the possibility of an attack on the new president increased. And the detective still didn't know how or when such an attack might come. But as he searched Baltimore's streets, alleys, and saloons for promising leads, Pinkerton was constantly reminded of the explosive fury of southern hatred for the

U.S. president-elect. Everywhere the detective heard men shouting for secession, cursing Lincoln, and threatening anyone who supported the federal Union. To Pinkerton, it seemed clear that a lot of Baltimore residents wanted the new president dead.

But after days of work, the detective still had no definite suspects. He had no concrete facts. And he had no proof that an actual plot to blow up railways or kill the president-elect even existed. The pressure to produce information was mounting, but the investigation seemed to have stalled. And then, just when it looked like he was really up against a wall, Pinkerton received a secret letter from one of Samuel Felton's railroad employees. The message read:

I am informed (by a reliable source) that a son of a distinguished citizen of Maryland said that he had taken an oath with others to assassinate Mr. Lincoln before he gets to Washington, and they may attempt to do it while he is passing over our (rail)road.

It was just a few words. But for Pinkerton, it was a start.

It confirmed that there was really a plot against the president-elect. But, more importantly, the letter had given the detective his first definite clue. By revealing that one of the plotters was the "son of a distinguished citizen," the secret message had narrowed the detective's search.

Instead of wasting time on investigations of poor and middle-class people, Pinkerton now knew that he should focus his search for potential assassins on the well-to-do members of Maryland's high society.

And, by chance, Pinkerton's agent Harry Davies had recently met a potential suspect who fit right into that group.

Otis Hillard, said Davies, was the gentleman's name.

He was a member of one of Baltimore's most important families. He sported one of the emblems of secession—a gold pin stamped with the picture of a palm tree—on the front of his jacket, and he was always eager to rant about how much he hated Lincoln. Hillard clearly had the money, the social connections, and the desire to organize an attack on the new president. So, Pinkerton's agent struck up a conversation with his suspect. He bought the man a few drinks, and he started to make friends.

At first, Hillard seemed suspicious and dodged Davies's questions. But soon the young man was babbling away as if Pinkerton's agent was an old, trusted pal.

Together the men discussed Lincoln, secession, and slavery—but Davies learned nothing new until Hillard started to jabber about belonging to a secret secessionist military society called the Palmetto Guards.

Sensing that he was on to something, Pinkerton's agent wanted to know more. But to do that, he had to get Hillard to open up. So—playing the part of a close friend—Davies invited his suspect out for a night on the town.

They had supper at Mann's Restaurant and played billiards at Harry Hemling's Billiard Room. Then it was on to the Pagoda Concert Saloon for a few drinks, and the two ended up at Davies's hotel room at around one a.m.

It had been a long, tiring evening. Over and over again, Davies had pressed for information, but Hillard hadn't said much that was useful. Then, as Pinkerton's agent was about to write off the night as a washout, Hillard asked if Davies had seen a copy of Lincoln's travel schedule.

Yes, the agent said, he had.

Well, Hillard chattered, "that reminds me that I must go and see a certain [person] in the morning. . . ."

About what? Davies pressed.

"About Lincoln's route . . . [and] Telegraphing."

Telegraphing? "How do you mean?"

Mellow, trusting, and probably a little drunk, Hillard explained that he and some others wanted to set up a telegraph code so they would know exactly where Lincoln was at any given time. "Supposing," said Hillard, "we should Telegraph to a certain point 'all up at 7,' that would mean that Lincoln would be at such a point at 7 o'clock."

It was late, but Davies was now wide-awake. Hillard was telling him about a secret code for tracking the newly elected president minute by minute. And the only reason a person like Hillard would need such a code was to plan an attack on Lincoln. This was hot stuff, and Davies began to ask Hillard for details about the plot.

Was there, he asked, a "plan of action" for dealing with the president-elect?

Yes, Hillard said. There was a plan.

But what kind of plan? Davies queried, hoping to pry loose a little more information.

But it was one question too many. Abruptly, Hillard clammed up. "My friend," he told Davies, "that is what I would like to tell you, but I dare not—I wish I could— anything almost I would be willing to do for you, but to tell you that I dare not."

It was Hillard's last word. But as his guest disappeared into the night, Davies knew he had made a giant breakthrough. In one evening, the agent had learned that there was definitely a plot. He had discovered the name of one of the conspirators. And he knew how the would-be attackers were tracking Lincoln's movements.

Quickly, Davies reported to his boss—and Pinkerton knew it was time to act. For the first time, he had evidence that the danger was real. Now, the detective had to warn Mr. Lincoln.

The question was: How?

To get the message there fast, he would have to use the telegraph. To make sure no dishonest telegraph operator leaked the information to the newspapers or to the conspirators, he would have to word the message very carefully. But to whom should he send the warning?

It had to be someone on the Lincoln team, someone who knew Pinkerton well enough to take his message seriously. But among Lincoln's traveling companions, there was only one person who fit the bill: Norman Judd. This black-eyebrowed, gray-bearded, cigar-chomping Illinois state senator was one of Lincoln's closest counselors. Rumors said that Mrs. Lincoln didn't like or trust Judd. But Norman Judd was an old friend of Pinkerton's, and he seemed like the perfect choice.

There was no time to lose, and on February 12, Allan Pinkerton ordered one of his agents to send a telegram to Mr. Judd. The dispatch, addressed to Norman Judd in Indianapolis, read:

I have a message of importance for you—where can it reach you by special Messenger. Allan Pinkerton.

For the moment the detective had done all that he could do. The message, encoded in dots and dashes, was on its way to Judd in Indianapolis. But would the new president's advisor get it? Would he take it seriously? And, when he learned the facts, would Judd convey the warning to Lincoln?

Chapter 8

WAITING FOR NEWS

Indianapolis, Indiana; Cincinnati, Ohio
February 12, 1861

It was February 12, Abraham Lincoln's fifty-second birthday, but he didn't have time for ice cream and cake.

At dawn huge crowds were already gathering in front of his Indianapolis hotel. Inside, the public rooms were clogged with people, and it seemed like all of Indianapolis had come to wave goodbye to the president.

Almost as soon as Mr. Lincoln got out of bed, he was whisked off to the state governor's house for breakfast. After coffee, he stopped at the state capitol building for a quick meet-and-greet session with lawmakers. Then it was back to the hotel, where he gave another short speech before dashing off to catch his eleven a.m. train.

All morning the president-elect's team hurried—making sure that Mr. Lincoln was where he was supposed to be, checking the schedule, and synchronizing watches. It was a crazy, busy time, and—right in the middle of all the fuss—someone handed presidential advisor Norman Judd a telegram.

Nobody sent telegrams unless the matter was urgent, and Judd wasn't expecting an emergency communication. Baffled, he scanned the paper. But the dispatch was brief and mysterious:

I have a message of importance for you—where can it reach you by special Messenger.   Allan Pinkerton.

Of course, Judd knew Allan Pinkerton well. But he couldn't imagine what this cryptic sentence meant or why the nation's leading detective needed to contact him immediately. The whole thing was very odd. Still, Judd knew that Pinkerton didn't play tricks, and any message from him had to be taken seriously. So, with that in mind, Lincoln's advisor quickly cabled back to meet him, "At Columbus the thirteenth—[or] Pittsburg the Fourteenth."

That took care of the immediate problem. Later, maybe, Mr. Judd would have time to think some more about the matter. But at the moment, he had to catch the train.

At the station there were more people—all hoping to see the president-elect or shake his hand. But once Lincoln climbed aboard, he found his wife and his two little sons, Willie and Tad, waiting to give him a hug.

Finally, the whistle shrieked. The clock struck eleven, and the red-white-and-blue train steamed out of the station. It was goodbye to Indianapolis and on to Cincinnati, Ohio, the next big stop.

For the passengers on the *Lincoln Special*, it was another long day of staring at the endless rolling countryside and waiting while the newly elected president gave short, unimportant speeches at little towns.

To entertain themselves, the two little boys played, squabbled, or thought up ways to tease their parents. Tad sometimes managed to be particularly irritating. At one stop, when the crowd asked to see him, the seven-year-old pretended to be shy, hid on the floor of the passenger car, and refused to come out.

Still, none of this appeared to bother Mr. Lincoln. Maybe he felt good because the sun was shining, because it was his birthday, or because his family was with him. Whatever it was, he seemed cheerful. And when the train roared into Cincinnati at three p.m., the president-elect must have been completely delighted to find that the citizens had gone all out to give him an over-the-top welcome.

So many people had turned out that soldiers had to

shoo crowds off the track so that the train could enter the station. Then, when Mr. Lincoln stepped out on the platform, the whole mob went wild. They cheered. They yelled. Over and over again they shouted for, "'the President' and the 'Union.'"

On the road to the hotel, almost every house was decorated with flags, banners, and anti-secession signs reading, "The American Union, forever" and "A union that nothing can sever." Several times the procession stopped briefly so that the new president could be toasted with a glass of beer or hear thirty little girls sing "The Star-Spangled Banner." And when Mr. Lincoln made a short speech saying that he hoped "our national difficulties will . . . pass away" and that all the differences between the North and the South would soon be "forgotten and blown to the winds forever," the crowd erupted with more cheers.

The rest of the evening disappeared in a cloud of handshakes and greetings. At last, however, Mr. Lincoln said a final good night to his advisors, opened the door to his hotel room, and spied young Tad. The little boy had tried to stay up late to see his father but instead had fallen asleep in a chair. Gently, the president-elect undressed his littlest son, carried him to bed, and tucked him under the covers.

Only then could Abraham Lincoln finally lie down himself. But as he took off his jacket and tie before going to sleep, a part of Mr. Lincoln's mind was probably wide-awake with worry.

All day people had cheered for him. All day people had called him "president." But the truth was: Abraham Lincoln hadn't officially been elected president—*yet*. And, what was more, he couldn't be officially elected president until the next day, February 13, when the last part of the complicated U.S. presidential election process would take place.

Despite the fact that Abraham Lincoln had won more votes than any other candidate on Election Day in November, those votes did not make him president. They did not make him president because the U.S. Constitution says that a U.S. president must be chosen not by the general public but by a special group of people called "electors."

Even today many don't realize that when they cast a ballot in a presidential election, they are not actually voting for the candidate. Instead, they are voting for a group of people called electors who have promised to support that candidate. This means that a person who voted for Abraham Lincoln in 1860 was actually voting not for Lincoln but for an elector who had promised to cast his electoral ballot for Lincoln and the Republican Party.

Under the electoral system—then and now—each state is allotted a certain number of electors; and, once those electors have been chosen, they vote. Their ballots are then counted in front of the entire Congress in Washington, D.C., and the candidate who gets the most votes becomes president of the United States.

As a rule, this process is pretty automatic. In most cases the candidate who gets the most popular votes on Election Day also gets the most electoral votes. But sometimes problems occur. And Abraham Lincoln knew that this time a lot of things could go wrong.

Because the country was divided and many Americans despised him, there was a chance that some electors had broken their promises and refused to vote for Lincoln. It was possible that some southerners in Congress might deliberately miscount the votes. Some citizens even feared that southern secessionists might try to march on Washington, seize the city, and prevent the votes from being counted. Any one of those events could throw the country into chaos. And any one could prevent Mr. Lincoln from becoming president.

The situation was both worrying and dangerous, but there wasn't much the president-elect could do about it. Whatever was going to happen would happen. But as he closed his eyes and drifted off to sleep, Abraham Lincoln may well have wondered if the next day he was going to be officially elected president of the United States.

And nearby, in another hotel room, the president-elect's close advisor Norman Judd may have been wondering too.

The next day or the day after that—on February 13 or 14—Judd was supposed to meet Pinkerton's special messenger. But why had the detective suddenly contacted him? Why was he acting so mysteriously? And what on earth was so secret and urgent about his news?

Norman Judd, an Illinois state senator
and one of Abraham Lincoln's closest advisors.

Chapter 9

DECISIONS

Cincinnati and Columbus, Ohio; Washington, D.C. February 13, 1861

"We Never Sleep" was the motto of the Pinkerton National Detective Agency, and Pinkerton agent William Scott was proving it true.

Since being ordered to deliver an urgent message to Norman Judd, Scott had traveled fast. After zipping across the country by train, he'd caught up with the Lincoln party early—meeting them in Cincinnati on the morning of February 13.

Judd had been fast asleep in his Cincinnati hotel room when the agent arrived at two a.m. At eight a.m., when the president-elect's advisor appeared, William Scott handed over Pinkerton's urgent letter and waited while Judd absorbed the contents.

In brief, the message said that Allan Pinkerton had discovered indications that "there was a plot on foot to assassinate Mr. Lincoln on his passage through [Baltimore]" and that the detective would soon provide more facts about the situation.

It was bombshell news. But Judd didn't look shocked. He didn't act upset. Nor did he seem particularly surprised. Instead, the new president's advisor quietly told Agent Scott that he was "very much obliged to you and A.[Allan] P.[Pinkerton]—for the information."

But surely Mr. Judd had questions. . . . Didn't he want to know more? Would he like Scott to contact Pinkerton immediately by sending a telegram in code?

"I think not," said Judd.

At the moment, it seemed best to wait for more details. And, in a way, that made sense. After all, Allan Pinkerton was completely trustworthy. He knew how to do his job. And for security reasons, it was important to keep this news confidential. Even a coded telegram could be intercepted and deciphered, and Judd didn't want information about a possible plot leaked to newspaper reporters or enemies.

Besides, Pinkerton might be wrong. The threat might not be real. And the whole thing might just blow over.

There were a lot of factors to consider, and Judd must have weighed various alternatives. But at some time before boarding the train that would take the new president's party to Columbus, Ohio, he apparently made his decision. For fear of "causing undue anxiety or unnecessary alarm," Judd decided *not* to tell the president-elect or any other member of his team about Allan Pinkerton's urgent warning. He decided *not* to tell them that there might be a real plot to murder Mr. Lincoln or that the new president might be attacked in Baltimore. To avoid causing an uproar, Norman Judd decided *not* to tell anyone that Abraham Lincoln's life might now be in very serious danger.

And on February 13, 1861, that probably seemed like a good idea. It seemed good to keep quiet about worrisome information—because at that moment almost every American was already on edge.

In the North, in the South, in the East, and in the West, everyone knew that February 13 was the day that the electoral votes for president would be counted in Congress. It was the day Congress was supposed to declare that Abraham Lincoln had been officially elected president. But no one knew if that was really going to happen, and all Americans were waiting for news from the capital.

Certainly, citizens in Washington were nervous. Although General Winfield Scott—the man in charge of city security—had sworn that any person who tried to disrupt the electoral vote would be "lashed to the muzzle of a [cannon] and fired out of a window of the Capitol," the air was thick with frightening rumors that southerners would stage riots, plant bombs, or launch attacks to prevent the electoral votes from being counted. Many cautious folks had already left town for safety, and those who remained saw that the Capitol Building (where Congress met) was surrounded by barricades of cannon and soldiers. An angry crowd occupied the long avenue linking the Capitol to the White House. There were street fights between Union supporters and secessionists all over town. And uniformed military men stood guard at the Capitol Building entrance to make sure that only U.S. senators, U.S. representatives, and special guests were allowed into the House of Representatives chamber to watch the vote.

Inside, the outgoing vice president, John Breckinridge, a tall, good-looking, square-jawed southerner, came forward to preside over the vote count.

Conversation ceased, and complete silence settled over the chamber as—one by one—the electoral votes were read out and tallied.

There were 12 votes for candidate Stephen Douglas, 39 votes for candidate John Bell, 72 for candidate John Breckinridge, and 180 electoral votes for Abraham Lincoln.

The results were in. The count had been witnessed by Congress. Now it was up to Vice President Breckinridge to certify the vote. But would he?

Breckinridge was a strong supporter of slavery. He had run against Lincoln in the presidential election, and he would soon serve the Confederacy as a general and secretary of war. In almost every way his political beliefs differed from Lincoln's. So would he now try to prevent a man he disagreed with from becoming president?

For one tense moment the assembled senators and congressmen waited. Then in a "clear," "strong" voice, the outgoing vice president began to speak.

"Abraham Lincoln of Illinois," he said, "having received a majority of the whole number of electoral votes, is duly elected President of the United States for the four years beginning on the fourth day of March, 1861."

It was done. Breckinridge—despite his personal beliefs—had done his public duty honestly and honorably. Abraham Lincoln was officially elected.

Reporters practically fell over one another in their rush to get the news to telegraph offices. Dit dah dah dit dit dit . . . the wires hummed as Morse code operators flashed the message around the country.

In Columbus, Ohio, Mr. Lincoln was meeting with yet another group of officials when someone handed him a telegram. It read, "The votes were counted peaceably. You are elected."

It was the news he'd been waiting for. But Abraham

Lincoln didn't shout or clap. Instead, he slowly smiled. He shoved the envelope in his pocket, and he continued to do the same things he'd been doing since leaving Springfield. He pushed through crowds where people were "packed together as closely as pickles in a jar." He let citizens shake both his hands with "frantic enthusiasm." And he made another dull speech.

"Citizens of Ohio," Mr. Lincoln said, "there is nothing going wrong. . . . We [the North and the South] entertain different views upon political questions, but nobody is suffering. . . . All we want [to solve our national problem] is time and patience. . . ."

It was the same standard, say-nothing-about-the-crisis speech he'd been making all along. But some people were getting tired of it.

"Nothing going wrong?" howled one New York newspaper. "Why, sir, we may more truly say there is nothing going right." And the newspaper had a point— because while Lincoln was making his namby-pamby, say-nothing speeches, the nation's problems were getting worse.

More and more southern states were thinking about leaving the Union. There was now even serious talk of secession in states located close to the northern border, like Maryland, Missouri, and Kentucky. As he traveled to his inauguration, Confederate president-elect Jefferson Davis constantly fueled fears by talking about the possibility of civil war. In a bloodthirsty, threatening speech, he told audiences that the "densely populated" cities of the North might soon be "food for the sword and torch" of southern armies.

Almost everywhere people were restless, angry, frightened, and looking for someone to blame. Some criticized outgoing U.S. president James Buchanan for letting the crisis over slavery develop in the first place. But others, like Pinkerton's prime Baltimore suspect, Otis Hillard, blamed the national breakup on the new president. "What a pity," Hillard complained, "that this glorious Union must be destroyed all on account of that monster Lincoln."

To Hillard, and others like him, it seemed that the problems of secession and slavery would vanish if Lincoln could be prevented from taking office.

But Abraham Lincoln had won the public election in November, and he'd won the February 13 electoral vote. Now, the only thing that could keep him out of the White House was . . . murder.

And suspect Otis Hillard, detective Allan Pinkerton, and presidential advisor Norman Judd all knew it.

John C. Breckinridge, Vice President of the United States from 1857-1861.

Although he was a pro-slavery southerner and Lincoln's political rival, Breckinridge did not try to overturn the 1860 election results. Instead, he officially certified the electoral vote that made Lincoln president.

Chapter 10

"LINCOLN SHALL DIE IN THIS CITY."

Baltimore, Maryland
February 15, 1861

In his years on the job, Allan Pinkerton had learned a lot from being a private eye. He'd learned about disguises. He'd learned how to track criminals. But most of all, he'd learned that the detective business was full of surprises. No one could ever predict which clue would pay off or where the next break might come from. So a good investigator had to be patient, persistent, and flexible enough to follow every lead. Success often depended on being able to change direction at a moment's notice, and that was exactly what Allan Pinkerton was doing now.

Just a few days earlier, the detective and Agent Harry Davies had felt that keeping a close eye on suspected plotter Otis Hillard was the most promising tack. But something new had turned up. And now it looked like one of Pinkerton's very first suspicions was about to bear fruit.

Back when he'd first moved into his Baltimore office and started to pose as John Hutcheson, a southern secessionist businessman, the detective had met a fellow building tenant named James Luckett. Since Luckett hated Abraham Lincoln, was a passionate believer in secession, and was well-connected in Baltimore social circles, Pinkerton suspected that the man might know something about a planned attack on the new president. Slowly and carefully, the detective had worked to win his neighbor's trust. He'd pretended to strongly support all Luckett's extreme views on secession, southern rights, and Abraham Lincoln. And he'd done the job well—so well that on February 15 Luckett took Pinkerton aside and began to pour out his feelings about politics.

Jumping from topic to topic in a confused, angry, rambling rant, Luckett told the detective that the only way to keep U.S. federal troops out of the South was for Virginia and Maryland to secede immediately. It was a pity, he said, that southerners hadn't already managed to seize the city of Washington, stop the electoral vote, and prevent Lincoln from officially becoming president. Still, Luckett said, he was sure that when Maryland and Virginia did secede, they would be able to stop any northern invasion by sending one hundred thousand men to surround the U.S. capital.

As the man babbled on, Pinkerton listened. He waited. He pretended to sympathize. And when Luckett paused, the detective pounced.

But what about Lincoln? Pinkerton asked.

What would happen if the new president tried to pass through Baltimore on his way to Washington?

Well, Luckett replied darkly, "He . . . *may pass through* [the city] *quietly but I doubt it.*"

But, Pinkerton responded, hadn't the local police marshal just publicly promised that Lincoln would get through Baltimore safely?

"Oh!" said Luckett, "That is easily promised, but may not be so easily done. . . ."

"Not so easily done"? Was Pinkerton hearing right? Was Luckett suggesting that Lincoln might actually be attacked in Baltimore? Did this ranting southern secessionist actually know of a plan to injure the president-elect? The detective had to find out. Somehow, he had to get Luckett to tell him more. To be more specific. To reveal everything he knew about a possible attack. And Pinkerton thought money might be a good persuader.

From his wallet, Pinkerton pulled out $25 and handed it to Luckett. The cash, he said, was to be used, "in the best manner possible" to support the cause of "Southern rights." Of course, the detective said modestly, he realized that his contribution was small. Still, it was a beginning; and Pinkerton hoped Luckett would feel free to ask him for more money or more help to defend the South.

Today, in twenty-first-century America, $25 may not sound like much—but in 1861 it bought about as much as $700 does now. Then, $25 was a lot of money, and Luckett was impressed. A man who gave so generously to support the South, secession, and slavery was surely a friend to be trusted, and in a burst of confidence, Luckett started to spill out sensitive information.

There was now a secret organization devoted to defending southern rights in Baltimore, he told the detective.

Luckett wasn't personally a member, but he knew the leader, Captain Cypriano Ferrandini. Although born in Italy, this Ferrandini was a "true friend to the South." He was ready to give his life to protect southern values, and he was going to make sure that Abraham Lincoln *never* reached Washington.

It was definitely Pinkerton's lucky day. New facts were falling into his lap like snowflakes falling in a blizzard. In just one brief conversation, he'd acquired evidence of a possible plot and learned the name of one of the possible plotters. After weeks of frustration, it was hard to believe things were going so well, but before the detective could mentally pat himself on the back, there was another surprise.

Luckett offered to introduce Pinkerton to Captain Ferrandini.

The detective jumped to accept, and the meeting was set for seven that evening at Barr's Saloon.

For Pinkerton, the rest of the day was uneventful. He had lunch. He spent some time in his office, and—as night fell—he made his way to the meeting place.

Inside, men were chatting and drinking. Luckett was already there, sitting with a handsome, intelligent-looking man whom he quickly introduced as Captain Cypriano Ferrandini.

Current events were on everyone's mind, and the conversation soon turned to politics. In his travels around Baltimore, Pinkerton had heard plenty of people rage about slavery, southern rights, secession, and how much they hated Lincoln, but Ferrandini was something different. When the Italian spoke about the South, "his eyes fairly . . . glistened . . . and his whole frame quivered" with passion. But Ferrandini was more than just a fanatic; he was a persuasive fanatic. When he talked, "faces . . . eagerly turned toward him," and Pinkerton noticed that the man seemed to have a "strange power" to influence others.

As the detective and other listeners gathered around, Captain Ferrandini told the spellbound group, "Murder of any kind is justifiable and right to save the rights of the Southern people." And the very first person southerners ought to murder was that evil monster . . . Abraham Lincoln.

"Never, never shall Lincoln be President," raved the Italian. A Lincoln presidency would be a disaster. It would destroy all the things that southerners cherished, and he, Cypriano Ferrandini, was now willing to die in order to "save" the South and kill the "Traitor" Lincoln.

Turning to Pinkerton, Ferrandini summed up his stand in a few forceful and terrifying words: *"If I alone must do it, I shall—Lincoln shall die in this City."*

And Lincoln was due to reach Baltimore in only eight days.

Chapter 11

"THERE IS NO CRISIS."

Various cities in Ohio and Pennsylvania
February 14-15, 1861

In Baltimore, Ferrandini was planning to kill the new president, but in Columbus, Ohio, Mr. Lincoln was trying to catch the eight a.m. train to Pittsburgh.

Overnight, the weather had turned nasty, and in Columbus it was a miserable morning. Rain was pouring down, and the president-elect had to push through a crowd of umbrellas to reach the *Lincoln Special*. Mrs. Lincoln and the boys arrived so late that they almost missed the train. And when the locomotive pulled out of the station, most of the passengers seemed cross and grumpy. To cheer up the party, one of Lincoln's old friends started a song. Others joined in, and soon everyone—including the new president—was singing.

Outside, the weather was still cold, gray, and wet. But even rain didn't keep crowds from turning out. At stop after stop, hundreds stood in the mud and the drizzle, waiting patiently to catch a glimpse of Mr. Lincoln and hear him say a few brief words.

Mostly, these people were satisfied if the president-elect waved, told a joke, or said a few words of thanks to his supporters, but at one stop an audience member had a different idea.

Abe! A coal miner called when the new president stepped out onto the railway car platform. "They say you're the tallest man in the United States, but I don't believe you're any taller than I am."

Well, Lincoln called back cheerfully, "come up here and let's measure."

As the crowd watched, the miner swung himself up to where the president-elect was standing. Then the two men stood back to back. Mr. Lincoln was six foot four in his socks, and the miner was pretty tall, too. Someone had to judge, so the new president asked one of his military advisors, Colonel Elmer E. Ellsworth, to take a look. But no matter how he stretched, the little colonel—who was just a little over five and a half feet high—couldn't see the very tops of the big men's heads. Still, Ellsworth was a resourceful man. As the crowd giggled, he climbed up high on a nearby railing. From there the short officer sized up the tall contestants and solemnly announced, "I believe they are exactly the same height." The whole audience cheered, and Lincoln said a warm goodbye to the miner with a smile and a handshake.

But aside from that pleasant moment, it was a difficult day. The weather was depressing. The train was late; and, because of a holdup on the line, the *Lincoln Special* didn't chug into Pittsburgh until eight that night—three hours after its planned arrival.

Tired and hungry, the president-elect and his team must have wanted nothing more than a hot dinner and a warm bed, but the pouring rain and the three-hour delay hadn't stopped the usual throng from turning out to see Mr. Lincoln. At the station, the crowd was so thick that soldiers were barely able to clear a path for the new president.

And when Mr. Lincoln himself stepped out on the platform, hundreds of voices began calling for a speech.

Speech!

Speech!

Another speech?

The president-elect had been giving short speeches at little whistle-stop towns all day. Probably the last thing he wanted to do was make another, but he didn't have much choice. Back in Springfield, Mr. Lincoln had decided to take this trip to introduce himself to America. He'd felt Americans were entitled to get to know just who and what he was. So now he was stuck. Standing up in his carriage, he said a few words of thanks to the enthusiastic residents of Pittsburgh and then promised to say more the following morning.

And sure enough, at eight a.m., Mr. Lincoln was standing on his hotel balcony, facing a crowd of five thousand rain-soaked citizens huddling under umbrellas. Some had just come to get a glimpse of the most famous man in America, but others were probably there because they wanted answers. They were tired of reading Mr. Lincoln's meaningless, dodge-the-issues speeches in the papers. They were hoping that this time he'd speak seriously about the nation's problems. And they weren't alone.

A lot of people in all parts of the country were getting pretty upset about the president-elect's refusal to discuss the issues. Some even suspected that he'd avoided talking about slavery and secession because he didn't have the brains or the guts to take on the country's biggest problems. And one of those people was U.S. congressman Charles Francis Adams.

As the son of U.S. president John Quincy Adams and the

grandson of U.S. president John Adams, the congressman considered himself an expert on proper presidential behavior—and he wasn't impressed with Mr. Lincoln's. The new president, Adams wrote in his diary, seemed to be a "good natured, kindly, honest" fellow. But Lincoln's toothless, say-nothing speeches simply showed that the president-elect was an intellectual lightweight who was too "frivolous and uncertain" to cope with his new job or understand the seriousness of the situation.

Of course, no one likes being criticized, but Mr. Lincoln generally didn't let faultfinders get under his skin. He was an old hand at dealing with critics, and he often managed to disarm them with a joke. Once, for example, when a political rival called him "two-faced," Lincoln replied, "If I had another face, do you think I would wear this one?" But jokes didn't work in all situations. So, most of the time, Mr. Lincoln just closed his ears and smiled at his critics. He did what he thought was right, no matter what people said, and he still believed that the right course was to hold his tongue, to see how the national situation developed, and to keep his real thoughts secret until the inauguration.

Then, on March 4, when he gave his top secret speech, he'd let loose. Yes. When he finally gave the speech that was locked in his little black satchel, he'd spill the beans. On that day, the whole country would know exactly where he stood on the issues. But in the meantime, he wasn't going to risk saying anything that might make matters worse.

So when impatient folks in Pittsburgh wanted to know why he hadn't yet presented a plan for dealing with the crisis, Mr. Lincoln said that he wanted to "give this subject all the consideration which I possibly can before I speak . . . definitely. . . ." And when they wanted to know what he thought of the "distracted condition of the country," Mr. Lincoln just said, "There is no crisis except an artificial one . . . gotten up . . . by turbulent men, aided by designing politicians. My advice, then . . . is to keep cool. If the great American people will only keep their temper on both sides of the line . . . the trouble will come to an end. . . . And this great nation shall continue to prosper. . . ."

Certainly, the words sounded nice—nice and comforting. Although most of the Pittsburgh crowd cheered, some probably frowned and shook their heads. Surely, sooner or later this new president was going to have to say something definite about the country's troubles. So why, they wondered, didn't he just get on with it? Why didn't he tell them what he thought about secession? Why didn't he say whether he favored war or peace? Why wouldn't he speak?

But now there was no time to ask those questions. The clock was ticking. Aides hustled the president-elect out of the hotel and down to the railway station. With the raindrops still trickling down, Mr. Lincoln stood by the engine shaking hands and kissing babies. Then, as the clock hands moved to ten a.m., the new president waved to the crowd one last time, and the *Lincoln Special* sped on to Cleveland.

In between stops there was nothing much for the passengers to look at except a cold, gray, wet landscape. But the relentless bad weather didn't stop the crowds. In the rain and mud, people stood at depots waiting for the *Lincoln Special*. And often, when the train pulled in, men and women begged to see both the president-elect and the new first lady. But Mrs. Lincoln was shy. As a rule, she couldn't be persuaded to go out and wave. So her husband laughingly told the crowds that "he had always found it very difficult to make her do what she did not want to do."

On and on the locomotive rumbled—stopping at this town, stopping at that town—as the long hours unspooled with ceaseless monotony. Once there was a little excitement when young Robert Lincoln sat next to the engineer and briefly tried to drive the train. Mrs. Lincoln chatted, the younger boys played, and for most of the trip the new president sat quietly by himself, staring into space or reading a newspaper.

It was turning into a long, dull day, and the president-elect's party was probably glad to get off the train for lunch in Alliance, Ohio.

Alliance wasn't big, but the citizens seemed determined to give the travelers a five-star welcome. A band entertained the new president with popular songs, a military unit stood guard, and the local hotel served up a delicious meal. Everyone was having a great time. Then, suddenly, there was an ear-splitting blast of gunfire. The dining room windows burst, and sharp fragments of glass rained over Mrs. Lincoln.

Was it an attack on the president-elect? For a moment, no one knew. Then, with relief, the Lincoln team realized it had been an accident. The explosion had been caused by soldiers who fired a ceremonial gun salute too close to the hotel.

No one was hurt, but the bang could have killed or injured the new president. Once again, events had shown just how easy it was to harm Mr. Lincoln, and that single fact should have frightened presidential advisor Norman Judd.

Two days had now passed since Agent William Scott had given Judd Allan Pinkerton's urgent warning. For two whole days Lincoln's advisor had known that there might be a real attempt to murder his boss in Maryland's biggest city. But for those two days Mr. Judd had ignored this possible crisis. In all that time he had not said a single word about the threat to the president-elect or any member of his team. And that was dangerous because with every passing day Mr. Lincoln was getting closer to Baltimore.

Chapter 12

A SITTING DUCK

Baltimore, Maryland
February 16, 1861

In Baltimore, Allan Pinkerton was on a roll. Suspect James Luckett had led him to Captain Ferrandini, and Ferrandini had openly admitted that he was planning to kill Abraham Lincoln. Evidence was steadily piling up, but the detective still didn't know one vitally important fact: He didn't know exactly how Ferrandini planned to commit the murder—and that was a crucial question.

In order to protect the president-elect, Pinkerton wanted to know exactly when, where, and how the attack would take place, so he decided to strike up another conversation with the talkative captain and persuade him to reveal additional details of the plot.

Since Ferrandini worked as a barber at Barnum's Hotel and the hotel lobby was a popular meeting spot for firebrand secessionists, Pinkerton figured it would be a good place to look for his quarry. Time, of course, was precious. So without wasting a moment, he headed for the corner of Fayette and Calvert Streets, entered the hotel, and found a seat in the busy lobby area.

Ferrandini didn't seem to be at the hotel that afternoon, but as Pinkerton cast his eye around the room, he spied Baltimore's police marshal, George P. Kane, talking with friends.

As chief of police, Kane would have the primary responsibility for protecting Lincoln in Baltimore. And the detective wanted to find out if this important man could be trusted to do the job.

Even without knowing the details of Ferrandini's plan, Pinkerton suspected that the attack would probably come when the president-elect was standing in a crowd at the railroad station or passing through the packed Baltimore streets during a parade. It would, the detective realized, be all too simple for a would-be assassin to slip into a throng of well-wishers, get close to Lincoln, and then pull out a knife or a gun. Or, alternatively, there was also the chance that Lincoln could be trampled, shot, or even blown up in the street by a violent, hostile Baltimore mob.

If Ferrandini and his associates were planning to strike by sneaking an assassin into a crowd or using mob violence, the president-elect would need heavy, top-notch police protection to get through Baltimore safely. But, although Police Marshal Kane had said publicly that he would provide guards for Lincoln, Pinkerton had his doubts.

Just the other day, when the detective had asked about Kane's public promise to protect the new president, suspect James Luckett had answered ominously, "Oh! That is easily promised, but may not be so easily done. . . ." Even more disturbing, however, was the fact that Kane and "the entire police force of the city" were known to be "in full sympathy with the [pro-slavery, secessionist] rebellion."

So, could pro-slavery, secessionist Kane be trusted to protect Lincoln? Pinkerton decided to listen to Kane's conversation to find out.

In the noisy, crowded room, it was hard to catch much of what the police marshal said. But the detective did hear Kane say that his department was *not* going to provide "a Police Escort for . . . ?" But—no matter how intently Pinkerton listened—he couldn't hear the words at the end of Kane's sentence. He couldn't tell exactly who or what the police marshal was refusing to protect. Still, the detective feared the worst. He feared Kane was telling friends that the Baltimore police force was not going to provide any security for Lincoln.

Without proper police guards, the new president would be a sitting duck. He would be completely at the mercy of would-be assassins like Ferrandini and the dangerous Baltimore mob.

It was a recipe for disaster, and Allan Pinkerton had to do something about it.

Chapter 13

"OUR SEPARATION FROM THE OLD UNION IS COMPLETE."

Montgomery, Alabama; various southern cities
February 16-18, 1861

Lincoln was not scheduled to arrive in Baltimore for another week, but Jefferson Davis, the new Confederate president, had almost reached his nation's first capital city: Montgomery, Alabama.

Since leaving his Mississippi plantation on the same day Lincoln left Springfield, Davis had roared through the South like a runaway rocket. In the five days it took to get from his home to Montgomery, the new president had stopped at Vicksburg, Jackson, Chattanooga, Atlanta, and plenty of small towns in between. In the process, he'd shaken so many hands, gone to so many receptions, and made so many speeches that most nights he'd just fallen asleep in his daytime clothes.

Still, it had been an exhilarating journey filled with crowds and cannon salutes. There had been folks who cheered when Davis said, "Our separation from the old Union is complete. NO COMPROMISE; NO RECONSTRUCTION CAN NOW BE ENTERTAINED." And when the new Confederate president swore that anti-secession northerners would "smell Southern [gun]powder [and] feel Southern steel," the local crowds went wild.

In those five days of travel, Davis had staked out his position. He had argued for the South's right to secede. He had affirmed the South's right to defend that stand. And, as he entered Montgomery, Alabama, at ten p.m. on Saturday, February 16, the only thing left was to swear his inauguration oath and restate those policies during his inaugural address the following Monday.

Certainly, the outlook seemed good when Inauguration Day, February 18, dawned bright and clear. Rooftops and windows around the Capitol bristled with curious spectators, and by noon several thousand people had gathered in front of the building to see Davis arrive in a carriage drawn by six white horses. Troops of soldiers in red and blue uniforms marched beside him, and crowds of enthusiastic ladies showed their admiration by pelting the new president with bouquets of sweet-smelling flowers.

Since no one had gotten around to writing a special southern patriotic song like "The Star-Spangled Banner" for the inauguration, a band played the stirring French national anthem. Of course, many in the vast audience had no idea what the words to that song were. But to knowledgeable French-speaking southerners, the French lyrics, which called for citizens to take up arms, march into battle, and overthrow tyrants, must have seemed perfect.

All in all, it was a grand day overflowing with music and cheers. But people had come to do more than just celebrate. They had come to hear Jefferson Davis deliver his inaugural address and see him sworn in as the first president of the new Confederacy.

Standing before the crowd on the steps of the Capitol Building, Mr. Davis spoke in a good, loud, "clear" voice that carried out to the edges of the crowd. Then, one by one, he made his points.

Once again, he told his audience that the southern states had a perfect right to leave the federal Union. The South, he said, had done no "wrong." Instead, the states had been forced to secede because of the North's aggressive and brutal attack on southern values—including slavery.

Now, Davis said, he hoped for peace. But he wanted the world to know that any attack on the Confederacy by the North would lead to "the suffering of millions" and show the "folly and wickedness" of the northern enemy.

The South would not fight "needlessly," the president declared. But if war came, the Confederate states would be ready. They would greet northern troops with a large, "well-instructed and disciplined army." And that army would fiercely defend the "honor and security" of the Southland.

Of course, along the way, the new nation would undoubtedly encounter problems. But, Davis believed, nothing would stop the progress of the blessed Confederate cause. Let us, he said finally, ask "the God of our Fathers" to "guide" the new nation "to success, to peace, and to prosperity."

The speech, at last, was over. Jefferson Davis had made his points. Then, as the crowd applauded, the new president turned to take his oath of office. Looking up toward heaven, with one hand raised and the other on the Bible, he swore to uphold the new Confederate constitution—a constitution that stated slavery could never be abolished in the South.

In his inaugural speech and tour, the new Confederate president had made his position clear. There was now no doubt that Jefferson Davis would fight to defend the

South's right to secession and slavery.

But what about Abraham Lincoln? Where did he stand on these issues?

It had been almost two months since the first southern state had seceded. In that time, Mr. Lincoln had not said one definite word about how he would handle the breakup of the Union. And the nation wanted to know.

So while white southerners cheered for Mr. Davis, other Americans were still waiting for the new U.S. president to speak.

Abraham Lincoln as he appeared just before the inauguration.
His right hand is closed due to the fact that it was badly swollen
from so much handshaking.

Chapter 14

A CLEAR-CUT SIGN OF TROUBLE

Buffalo, Albany, and other cities in New York State
February 16-18, 1861

Since leaving Springfield five days before, the new U.S. president had been busy. He'd shaken thousands of hands. He'd ducked questions about the state of the country. He'd talked himself hoarse, and he'd developed a fine routine for greeting crowds at the little whistle-stop stations along the way.

Generally, when the train stopped at a small town, Mr. Lincoln would pop out on the rear platform of his railway car, doff his hat, smile, and greet the crowd. Of course, he'd already made up his mind not to discuss serious matters until the inauguration, but he knew that most people liked to laugh. So, instead of long political speeches, the new president gave them jokes.

On the rare occasions when he could coax his shy wife to join him, the enormously tall president-elect would stand next to tiny Mrs. Lincoln. Then he'd make the crowd chuckle by saying that he was giving them "the long and the short of it." But sometimes he'd just poke fun at his own homely face by saying, "I have come to see you and allow you to see me and in this . . . I have the best of the bargain. . . ." Once, however, Lincoln got carried away. He spent so much time telling a funny story that the train pulled away before he finished. But since the joke sounded really good, some folks drove to the next town just to hear him deliver the punch line.

Mostly audiences loved the wisecracks and stories— partly because they were funny and partly because they made Lincoln seem like a regular, down-to-earth guy. But, of course, some sober-sided people objected.

One New York newspaper even published an article comparing the two new American presidents. Jefferson Davis, they said, was a dignified, serious leader who discussed the issues. But Lincoln? Lincoln, the paper commented, was nothing but a low-life "story teller and . . . joke maker." It was a nasty remark, but the new U.S. president didn't care. Lincoln liked making other people laugh. He liked telling stories. And on February 16 he told one about an entirely new topic: his beard.

"Some three months ago," Mr. Lincoln told a crowd in Westfield, New York, "I received a letter from a young lady here. It was a very pretty letter, and she advised me to let my whiskers grow, as it would improve my appearance. Acting partly upon her suggestion, I have done so; and now if she is here, I would like to see her."

As everyone watched, an old man led a twelve-year-old girl named Grace Bedell forward. Immediately, Mr. Lincoln stepped down from the train and held out his hand to her. "You see," the president-elect said, "I have let these whiskers grow for you, Grace."

Newspapers flashed the story around the country. Tens of thousands chuckled over it. Grace Bedell became famous. And Mr. Lincoln sped on to his next big stop: Buffalo, New York, the tenth-largest city in the United States.

By now, the Lincoln team had seen a lot of crowds. They'd seen little crowds. They'd seen big ones. But the crowd in Buffalo was *gigantic*. Ten thousand people were waiting at the depot. Even more jammed the streets. And when Mr. Lincoln got off the train, a mass of over-enthusiastic citizens rushed the new president. Almost overwhelmed by the mob, the Lincoln party "had to struggle with might and main for their lives," while all around the president-elect, "women fainted, men were crushed . . . and many others had their bones broken." Soldiers and members of the Lincoln team desperately struggled to protect their boss, but "the pressure was so great . . . that they were almost trampled to death." One of the new president's aides even had his shoulder dislocated in the violent scuffle.

By some miracle, Mr. Lincoln made it to his hotel in one piece. But the Buffalo riot was another terrifying reminder that the president-elect's life was not safe. Still, if Mr. Lincoln was alarmed by the violence, he didn't show it. Instead, he thanked the citizens of Buffalo for what he politely called a "grand reception," gave his usual say-nothing speech, and finally retired to get a little sleep.

The next day was Sunday, but for the exhausted Mr. Lincoln, even that wasn't a day of rest. With his hand sore from shaking and his voice worn to a rasp, the president-elect sat quietly through two church services. But he still had to make polite conversation during a dinner with former U.S. president Millard Fillmore, drag himself back to the hotel, and get up at four a.m. Monday morning to catch a train to Albany, New York's capital city.

It was another long day. Another long journey. And when the locomotive pulled into the Albany depot at two-thirty p.m., another huge crowd surged toward the train. Folks screamed, "Show us the Rail Splitter" and "Trot out Old Abe." Men and boys pushed past a police patrol and tried to climb on the cars. Inside their compartment, Lincoln and his team waited until an armed regiment of soldiers pushed through the crowd, drove off the toughs, and escorted the presidential party to their carriages.

Soldiers and police lined the streets to protect the president-elect. But a drunk pushed past the guards and raced up to Lincoln's carriage. For one heart-stopping moment, it looked as if the man was going to pull a gun on the new president. But the drunk, a Lincoln supporter, only wanted to grab his hero's hand and shake it vigorously.

Police finally dragged the man away, and the president-elect went on with the usual rounds. He met the mayor. He met the governor. He attended three state dinners. He shook hands. He patted babies. And, of course, he made another speech. But many noted that Lincoln looked tired. The crowds were exhausting, and the trip was taking a toll. Besides, he had a lot on his mind. In two short weeks he was going to take on the awesome responsibility of being president of the United States, and just that day he had received an unsettling reminder that almost half the country's citizens hated him.

While meeting with the governor of New York State, the president-elect had received a letter from one of his few southern supporters. It said that Lincoln's Maryland allies had regretfully decided that it would be unsafe and "inadvisable" to stage a big public welcome for the new president in Baltimore. Most of the city's population supported secession, detested the president-elect's views on slavery, and personally loathed him. Since the "City Authorities" were also "hostile," Mr. Lincoln would have no police protection in Baltimore and might be torn to pieces by an angry mob.

The note was a warning. An alarm bell. A clear-cut sign of trouble. But—even after reading it—Lincoln still didn't know just how serious the situation was in Maryland. Thanks to the letter, he knew he might have to face mob violence in Baltimore, but he didn't know that a dedicated band of assassins was planning to murder him there. And he didn't know for a reason.

Despite the fact that Lincoln had almost been injured by several friendly crowds in northern cities . . .

Despite the scary letter predicting mob violence in Baltimore . . .

And despite the fact that he'd recently received a message from Pinkerton saying that "evidence [of a murder plot] was accumulating," Norman Judd *still* had not told anyone in the Lincoln party about the detective's warning.

And the president-elect was due to arrive in Baltimore in just five days.

Chapter 15

EIGHT RED CARDS

Baltimore, Maryland
Sometime around February 17, 1861

One by one the puzzle pieces were falling into place. Over the past few days, Pinkerton had established that Ferrandini and his associates were planning to murder Abraham Lincoln. He was fairly certain they would attack when the president-elect tried to pass through the crowd at the Baltimore train station, but one important fact was still missing. Despite his best efforts, the detective still didn't know exactly who would commit the crime.

Would it be Ferrandini himself? Would it be one of the

other conspirators? Or would the strike be carried out by a group?

Knowing this key fact would help Pinkerton protect the new president. But how could he find out? There were several possibilities.

First, there was suspect James Luckett. Could he possibly provide the missing information?

No. Probably not. Luckett certainly knew Ferrandini, but the Baltimore businessman didn't seem to be a member of the captain's inner circle, so it wasn't likely he'd have access to any sensitive inside information. Luckett seemed to be out of the running.

But what about Ferrandini? Could Pinkerton persuade the captain to reveal the assassin's identity?

Again, unlikely. The detective had met Ferrandini only once, and the captain was not likely to divulge a crucial secret to a casual acquaintance.

So that left one other potential prospect: Otis Hillard.

Hillard, after all, had been the first to reveal the existence of a plot to murder Lincoln. He'd been able to tell Agent Davies that the conspirators had a telegraph code for tracking the president-elect's movements. And he'd hinted at having more information.

Yes. Evidence showed that Hillard belonged to Ferrandini's society. As a member he'd know the society's secrets. And since the young secessionist now viewed

Davies as a friend, Pinkerton's agent might well be able to pry a few more facts out of him.

And there was something else. In the past few days, Hillard and Davies had become almost inseparable. They'd visited each other, eaten meals together, and spent plenty of time drinking at Baltimore's fancy bars and saloons. So it was no surprise when Otis Hillard turned up at Davies's hotel room one afternoon and found the Pinkerton agent stretched out of the bed with a solemn, "sober" look on his face.

"What's the matter with you?" Hillard asked his friend.

"I am thinking about what a . . . tumult this country is in," replied Davies. "I have all kinds of bad thoughts shot through my mind—you know you can't prevent a man from thinking."

"Of course not," said Hillard. "What have you been thinking about?"

"I was thinking," said Davies, "if a man had the [nerve] . . . he could immortalize himself by taking a knife and plunging it to Lincoln's heart. . . ." But, the agent added sadly, "it is impossible to find a man with the pluck to do it."

Hillard, however, disagreed. No, he told his friend. "There are men who would do it. . . . If our Company would draw lots to see who would kill Lincoln, and the lot should fall on me, I would do it willingly. . . ."

Draw lots?

Do it willingly?

The words rang alarm bells in Davies's head. Was Hillard suggesting that the society was ready to choose an assassin? Instantly, the agent wanted to know more— but he had to be careful. A pushy question or an unwise remark might scare off Hillard. Even an overeager attitude might give the game away. Still, Davies was an experienced detective. He'd done tricky interviews before. And now he knew that the best plan was to stay cool, lead the conversation in a promising direction, and pray that his suspect would open up.

"You know," Davies fibbed casually, "I . . . have no desire . . . to ask you questions about your Company [except for the fact] that I of course feel an interest in this cause . . . being a Southern man."

It was a good hint. A nice try. But Hillard shied off. Instead of taking the bait, the young secessionist turned away. "I have told you all I have a right to tell you . . . ," Hillard said, and cut off the conversation.

Still, Davies persisted. That night over dinner in a private room at Mann's Restaurant, he brought up the subject again. But Hillard was touchy, nervous, and wary. "We have to be careful," he told Davies. "Do not think my friend that it is a want of confidence in you that makes me so cautious, it is because I have to be. . . . We have taken a solemn oath [not to] reveal any orders received by us, or entrusted to us, or anything that is confidential."

It was Hillard's last word on the subject. The talk turned to other things. To Davies, another try didn't seem practical. But when they discussed the matter, Pinkerton wasn't so sure. Hillard was still their best lead, and the detective hated to give up. Maybe with a little more effort Davies could worm something useful out of Hillard.

Of course, the job wouldn't be easy, but Pinkerton had faith. Davies was one of his best men, and he almost always came through with the goods. And this time—as usual—Davies didn't disappoint.

Although there is no record of how he did it, somehow the agent managed to win Hillard's trust. Somehow, in almost no time, Davies was able to convince Hillard of his desire to join Ferrandini's secret society. And late one afternoon, Hillard "joyfully informed" Davies that Ferrandini had agreed to make the agent a member. The initiation was scheduled to take place immediately, and that night Hillard led his trusted new friend through the shadowy Baltimore streets to the door of a large house.

Inside, about twenty men stood waiting in a curtained, dimly lit drawing room. But despite their numbers, the men were "strangely silent" as Hillard escorted Davies through the crowd and up to the place where Captain Ferrandini was stationed. Then, as the group looked on, Davies took a solemn oath of allegiance to the society and was warmly welcomed into the fellowship with handshakes from the other members.

With the formalities over, it was time for the real business of the meeting to get under way. Quiet again settled over the room, and Captain Ferrandini took the floor to explain exactly how the attack on the president-elect would be carried out.

As Pinkerton had suspected, the strike would come when Lincoln arrived at the crowded Baltimore railroad station. A few token policemen would be on duty, but they had already been ordered to do nothing that would protect the new president from violence. With only his advisors for guards, Lincoln would then be forced to make his way through a "dense, excited" "hostile crowd," and the "fatal blow" would be "struck" as the enraged mob pushed and jammed against him.

The plan was solid. The arrangements seemed foolproof. And this very night the society would choose the assassin. They would, said Ferrandini, choose the lucky man who would finally free "the nation of the foul presence of the abolitionist leader."

It would, the captain explained, be a fair and simple process. Each man in turn would blindly draw a slip of paper from a wooden box, and the man who found himself holding a red slip would be the designated murderer. Secrecy, however, was paramount. To keep the chosen assassin's identity safe, the selection process would be carried out in darkness. Faces would be hidden by the deepest shadows, and in the nighttime gloom, no one would be able to see the color on another man's paper lot. But, Ferrandini felt, even those precautions weren't enough. So, to ensure that no one would ever—even accidentally—disclose the true name of the murderer, all members would have to swear not to reveal the color of their cards before drawing lots.

The measures seemed sensible, and no one argued. Instead, each member groped his way forward through the darkness, thrust a hand into the wooden box, and withdrew a paper slip. One by one the men glanced at their cards in silence. Nobody broke the oath. Nobody revealed who had been chosen. But Davies was convinced that Ferrandini had placed not one but eight red cards in the box. Eight scarlet cards. Eight chosen assassins. With each assassin certain that he—and only he—was duty-bound to kill the president-elect. If one man failed, another would try—over and over, again and again—until Abraham Lincoln lay stone dead on the pavement.

The stage was set. The plot was in motion. Now only Allan Pinkerton and his agents could prevent disaster—and the detective was ready. "I resolved," said Allan Pinkerton, "to act at once."

Astor House, New York, NY, almost fifty years after Lincoln's visit at a time when it was no longer the city's most elegant hotel.

Chapter 16

A MESSAGE FOR MR. JUDD

Baltimore, Maryland; Albany, New York;
New York City
February 18-19, 1861

The sun had barely peeked over the horizon, but Allan Pinkerton was already on the move. Now that he knew all the details of the plot, the detective had to find a way to protect Mr. Lincoln. And early in the morning of February 18, Mr. Pinkerton was busy working out a plan.

First, he had to check the president-elect's published travel schedule to confirm dates and places. According to that timetable, Mr. Lincoln and his team would be arriving in New York City on Tuesday, February 19—the following afternoon. After that, they would move to Philadelphia on February 21, and then travel on until they reached Baltimore on February 23. Scheduling would be tight, but Pinkerton figured he had just enough time to get a preliminary message through to Norman Judd in New York City, put himself on a train to Pennsylvania, and then meet the new president's advisor in Philadelphia for a complete planning session on February 21. That took care of step one.

Step two was writing a message to Norman Judd. In it, the detective confirmed the existence of the plot, provided updated details about the attack, and told Judd to meet him in Philadelphia on the twenty-first. At that time, Pinkerton said, the two men could finalize the details of a scheme for getting the president-elect through Baltimore safely.

The message, of course, was secret—too secret to send by telegraph—and too urgent to put in the mail. Only a special messenger could be trusted to deliver it. And Pinkerton had already chosen the courier. It would be Agent Kate Warne, the brave, trusted, highly intelligent head of his female detective division.

Since coming to Baltimore, Mrs. Warne had spent most of her time gossiping with secessionist ladies in a boardinghouse as she tried to pick up clues about anti-

Lincoln activities in the city. So far, she hadn't learned anything particularly useful, but when Allan Pinkerton unexpectedly stopped by after breakfast on the morning of February 18, Kate Warne probably guessed that she was about to get a new assignment.

After making sure that their conversation could not be overheard, the detective pulled out the letter to Judd. He passed it to Mrs. Warne, briefed her on events, and instructed her to catch the 5:16 p.m. train to New York City. After arriving, she was to rent a room at the Astor House hotel, wait for the Lincoln party to check in there the following afternoon, and immediately deliver the letter to Norman Judd.

Of all Pinkerton's agents, Kate Warne was one of the most reliable. Mrs. Warne, he said, "never let me down." So, as expected, she quickly understood the details of her mission.

After paying her boardinghouse bill, tossing a few items in a suitcase, and tucking the all-important letter into a secure place, she headed for the railroad station. And when the 5:16 train to New York began its long, tedious, eleven-hour journey north, Kate Warne was on it.

The clocks were striking four a.m. when the train from Baltimore finally pulled into the New York depot. The sun had not yet risen, but Agent Warne found a horse-drawn cab and directed the driver to take her through the still-dark streets to Astor House, one of the city's fanciest hotels.

With her bag in hand, Pinkerton's agent made her way through the hotel's elaborate columned entryway, walked through the lobby, and asked for accommodations. It was a simple request, and it shouldn't have been a problem. Astor House, after all, had about three hundred rooms. But for some unknown reason, the management gave Mrs. Warne a hard time. Unwilling to take "no" for an answer, the agent persisted, and she was finally able to lie down in an Astor House bed just as dawn was breaking.

Tired but unable to sleep, she was up again at seven thirty a.m. and ready for work. But Lincoln's party wasn't due to reach the hotel until late afternoon, and in the meantime, she could do little except pace the floor, stare at the urgent letter, and watch for the arrival of the president-elect and Mr. Judd.

For Agent Warne, it was going to be a long, frustrating day. And for the new president's party, the outlook wasn't much better.

At this point, Abraham Lincoln had been on the road for eight days. For over a week he'd endured late nights, early mornings, long journeys, endless speeches, and exhausting bouts of handshaking. And when he got up at seven a.m. on Tuesday, February 19, the president-elect didn't feel well. Somehow, though, he managed to struggle into his clothing, pick up the black satchel containing his inauguration speech, and climb aboard the orange-painted, flag-decorated train that would carry him from Albany to New York City.

Even back in 1861, New York was one of the nation's biggest, most important cities, but Mr. Lincoln probably wasn't looking forward to his visit. And it was no secret that a lot of the city's residents disliked him.

The problem had come about because many New Yorkers made their living by doing business with the South. Some shipped and sold southern crops. Others made and sold supplies that southerners wanted to buy. But when the southern states seceded, southerners immediately stopped trading with New York. When North–South commerce ceased, many New York businessmen went broke and lots of New York workers lost jobs. Many suffered. And so many were affected by the business slump that New York City mayor Fernando Wood spoke out. He suggested that to save its merchants and workers the city should leave the Union, side with the South, and join the new Confederacy. That hadn't happened, but most New Yorkers blamed the new president for causing the secession trouble, and he was likely to get a very cold reception in the city.

Still, the scheduled visit had to be made, and as the train pulled into the station, Mrs. Lincoln tried to cheer up her husband by giving him a kiss.

The secessionist mayor of New York wasn't on hand to greet the president-elect, so the city's police chief escorted Mr. Lincoln out to an open carriage drawn by six magnificent black horses. To protect the nation's incoming president from possible mob violence, one squadron of police marched in front of the Lincoln procession, another police squadron marched behind it, and an additional thirteen hundred policemen lined the three-and-a-half-mile-long parade route.

Although thousands had turned out to see the president-elect, this time there were no cheers, no brass bands, no waving handkerchiefs, and almost no red-white-and-blue decorations. Instead the "vast" crowd was "silent" as Lincoln politely smiled and bowed. In other cities he had seen signs saying things like, "Honor to a President" and "The American Union, forever," but in New York one banner hanging outside a store seemed to sum up the feelings of the city. "Welcome, Abraham Lincoln," it read. "We beg for compromise."

Steadily the procession wound its way from the uptown station at Thirtieth Street down to lower Manhattan, but it was nearly four p.m. when Kate Warne saw the president-elect get out of his carriage at the hotel. To her, Lincoln looked "very pale and fatigued" as he arrived at the head of a string of thirty-five coaches. When she felt sure that everyone had settled in, Mrs. Warne penned a note to Judd, asking him to come to her room as soon as possible. Then she handed the note to a bellboy, told him to deliver it to the new president's advisor "immediately," and settled down to wait.

Within minutes the boy was back to report. There was, he said, no one named Norman Judd with the Lincoln party. There was no one named Norman Judd at the Astor House hotel. And—though the bellboy didn't know it—at that moment, there was no one named Norman Judd in all of New York City.

Mr. Lincoln's close personal advisor had missed the morning train.

Mary Todd Lincoln

Chapter 17

TEN-TO-ONE ODDS

New York City
February 19-20, 1861

The regularly scheduled train from Albany was slow, and the clock hands were pointing to six thirty p.m. when Norman Judd finally walked through the front door of New York's Astor House hotel. After a long, trying day of travel and missed connections, he probably could have used some rest and relaxation. But before he could unpack or put up his feet, Judd had to talk to a general. And while the president-elect's advisor was involved in that conversation, a bellboy handed him a note. It said that a lady in another room wanted to see him as soon as possible. Exactly who this strange lady was or what she wanted to see him about, Judd didn't know. Still, he followed the messenger to a room on one of the hotel's upper floors and knocked at the door. When he entered, a slim young woman rose from her chair. "Mr. Judd, I presume?" she said. "Yes, madam," a puzzled Judd responded. But before he could say much more, Kate Warne explained that she had come to New York to give Judd a message so urgent that it could not be sent by mail. Then she handed him Pinkerton's note.

Faced with a letter containing a mysterious, possibly alarming message, Judd apparently felt that he needed something to settle his nerves. He politely asked Mrs. Warne if he could smoke. Then, with a cigar clamped between his lips, Mr. Judd ripped open the envelope, read the letter—and suddenly understood three terrible things:

One—the plot against the president-elect was real.

Two—the threat was immediate.

Three—for days, he, Norman Judd, had ignored this awful, looming danger.

Upset and obviously unsure of what to do, Mr. Judd began firing off questions. Could Mrs. Warne rush a letter to Baltimore for him? Could Pinkerton meet him in New York right away? Could he show the detective's letter to all the other members of the Lincoln team? Could he consult the New York City police about the problem?

The new president's advisor sounded panicky, but the Pinkerton agent was completely in charge.

In a calm, controlled way, Mrs. Warne reassured Judd and answered his questions.

Yes. She could leave early in the morning to take a letter to Pinkerton.

No. Allan Pinkerton couldn't possibly reach New York before Judd had to leave with the Lincoln party.

And no, Norman Judd definitely could not show the letter to anyone else on the president-elect's team or to the New York City police.

Because southern spies might now be watching the Lincoln party, secrecy had to be absolute. It was important to make sure that no one on the team accidentally said or did anything that might let the conspirators know that their plans had been uncovered. At this point, the fewer people who knew about the plot, the better.

Besides, Warne added, Judd had to remember that Allan Pinkerton was on the job, and America's number one detective was not going to let anything happen to the new president. All Judd had to do right now was to "keep cool," say nothing, and meet Mr. Pinkerton in Philadelphia on February 21.

As Mrs. Warne talked and the evening went on, Judd seemed to relax. Soon, he was acting normally. And when he said good night at eleven thirty, the president-elect's advisor was composed enough to chat about how embarrassing it had been to miss the morning train and how "tickled to death" Mrs. Lincoln had been by all the interesting things she'd seen since leaving home.

For Kate Warne, it had been a good but exhausting day. She'd accomplished everything she'd needed to—but, though it was almost midnight, she wasn't quite finished. Before turning in, she asked the hotel staff to wake her in time to catch the early train to Baltimore. Then, at last, she tumbled into bed, feeling very "tired."

Judd was probably tired too. But although Mrs. Warne had assured him that Allan Pinkerton had matters well in hand, the new president's advisor must have been worried: worried about the danger, worried that he hadn't acted sooner, and worried about whether the detective's plan could save the president-elect.

Still, Judd did as he'd been told. If he had worries, he kept them to himself. And when the morning sun filtered through the curtains at Astor House, Abraham Lincoln didn't know anything about a plot, about Pinkerton, or about a serious threat to his life. He only knew that at eleven o'clock he was supposed to meet Mayor Fernando Wood at City Hall.

Just the day before, New York's mayor had insulted the president-elect by not greeting him personally at the railway station. Now, as he faced the nation's new chief executive, the mayor was rude again. Instead of giving Mr. Lincoln a warm, gracious welcome, Mayor Wood began to publicly lecture the president-elect on the welfare of New York. Since the business success of the city depended on having a united country, he ordered Mr. Lincoln to do whatever it took to bring back the seceded states and restore the federal Union.

It was a crude, blunt demand, but Lincoln's response was polite. "There is nothing," he said carefully, "that could ever bring me to consent—willingly consent—to the destruction of the Union. . . ." And he said it with such firmness and force that even his critics were impressed.

The discussion, however, couldn't go on much longer. Outside City Hall, five thousand people were waiting to greet the new president. So for the next several hours Mr. Lincoln shook hands with his admirers, told jokes, and made small talk.

One visitor from New Jersey walked up, took a look at the president-elect, and said, "I have been told I look like you." Well, Lincoln shot back, "You do look like me, that's certain. The fact is settled that you are a handsome man."

By one o'clock the handshaking marathon was over, but Lincoln still had other items on the agenda. He had to meet a ninety-four-year-old man who had voted for George Washington in America's first presidential election. And he also had to accept presents from two different New York hatters.

In the gift boxes were three pieces of headgear. Two were Mr. Lincoln's usual tall stovepipe hats. But the third was a soft, wide-brimmed cap that looked a little like a cowboy hat. Of course, both manufacturers wanted one of their hats to be the new president's favorite. But Mr. Lincoln—as always—was tactful. The hats "mutually surpass each other," he said.

For Lincoln, it was a pretty standard working day. But while the president-elect shook hands and made speeches, his family found time for a visit to one of New York's hottest attractions: Barnum's American Museum.

The museum, founded by America's greatest showman, P. T. Barnum, was part zoo, part circus, and part oddity collection. For the 25-cent price of admission, visitors could see such wonders as a live whale, the "Fejee mermaid" (a hideous fake mummy made of a monkey's head and a fish body), and the "Lightning Calculator," a man who could instantly add up long columns of huge numbers in his head. There were tanks of tropical fish, a bearded lady, waxworks, a glassblower, a trapeze performer, and cases filled with sharks' teeth, petrified pork, lace from George Washington's carriage, and a "Ball of Hair" found in the stomach of a sow.

Nobody knows what the president-elect would have

thought of these weird, wacky exhibits, but Tad had an opinion. He absolutely did not want to see the museum's two-thousand-pound "Great Grizzly Mammoth Bear Samson." A two-thousand-pound grizzly must have sounded pretty scary, and the little boy said he'd already seen a lot of real, live bears at home.

Although Tad and the other boys might have liked to spend the evening with their dad, the president-elect had other things to do. At six p.m., dressed in his evening clothes, Abraham Lincoln was on the move again. This time he escorted his wife to a private dinner with the new U.S. vice president, Hannibal Hamlin, and Mrs. Hamlin.

Everyone apparently got on well, and the foursome chatted as waiters served chicken in truffle sauce, roast quail, and French pastries. However, when plates of baked oysters were brought in, Mr. Lincoln seemed a little doubtful. Since he'd spent most of his life far from the ocean on the midwestern prairies, the new president probably hadn't had the chance to eat much seafood. So he gave the grayish blobby oysters a good hard look. "I don't know that I can manage these things, but I guess I can learn," he said.

After dinner, it was on to the opera, where New York's richest, most stylish, most sophisticated citizens were waiting to have a look at Mr. Lincoln. And some of them weren't impressed.

First, there was the new president's backwoods accent. He said "thar" instead of "there." He said "heered" instead of "heard," and the word "education" came out as "eddication."

Then there was his appearance. No matter how expensive they were, clothes hung on his tall, gangly body like black rags on a flagpole. One reporter noted that when the president-elect strode along with his legs moving and his arms waving, he looked like the combination of a "derrick and a windmill." His face was homely. His hair was always mussed. His beard seemed scraggly. But to fancy New York opera-goers, the worst thing of all was the new president's gloves.

In 1861, well-mannered gentlemen were supposed to wear white kid gloves to the opera. But instead of white gloves, Mr. Lincoln had put a pair of black kid gloves on his giant hands. And the elegant New York audience was appalled. One visiting southern gentleman sarcastically said that those black gloves made Lincoln look like an "undertaker"—"the Undertaker of the Union."

It was a mean comment—and it was also untrue.

The president-elect wasn't trying to bury the Union. But Ferrandini and his fellow conspirators were trying to bury the new president.

That night, as the unsuspecting Mr. Lincoln sat listening to music, southern newspapers were reporting that a huge sum of money had been offered to anyone who would assassinate the president-elect before the inauguration. And in Baltimore, gamblers were busy. At ten-to-one odds, they were betting that someone was going to murder Abraham Lincoln. In their city. Very, very soon.

General Winfield Scott, the U.S. Army commander in charge of security in Washington who, along with other officials, hired a New York detective to investigate the possibility of an attack on Abraham Lincoln in Baltimore.

Chapter 18

"FIND MR. LINCOLN."

Washington, D.C.
Morning and early afternoon, February 21, 1861

There was a plot? A plot to murder Abraham Lincoln?

It was early morning. U.S. colonel Charles Stone was barely awake, and New York City detective David Bookstaver had just burst into his room like ten tons of TNT.

Weeks ago, General Winfield Scott, chief of the U.S. government's military branch, and several other U.S. officials had become deeply concerned about the new president's safety. None of them knew anything about Pinkerton's activities, but Washington was full of rumors about assassination plots. It was hard to tell if the danger was real or imaginary. So Scott and his colleagues had secretly hired Detective Bookstaver to investigate possible threats to Mr. Lincoln.

Now Bookstaver had come to report his findings to General Scott's assistant, Colonel Stone, and the policeman's account was shocking.

For almost a month, Bookstaver—who also knew nothing about the Pinkerton project—had been investigating anti-Lincoln activity in Baltimore. Like most detective work, it had been difficult, dangerous, and frustrating. But the day before the detective had struck gold. He'd found a piece of important evidence. Now, like Pinkerton, he had proof—positive proof—that secessionists were planning to murder Lincoln when the president-elect stepped off the train in Baltimore on February 23. It was terrifying news, but Stone had no authority to act on it. He immediately rushed Bookstaver's report to his boss, General Scott.

Scott was seventy-four years old, ill, enormously fat, and such a fuddy-duddy that some people called him "Old Fuss and Feathers." But despite his age, his health, and the fact that he was a born southerner, Scott was dedicated to his job and devoted to the U.S. government. He felt personally responsible for Lincoln's safety, and he rapidly realized that someone had to travel north to warn the new president. The problem was: Who would do it?

It had to be someone loyal. Someone Mr. Lincoln knew. Someone whose opinion the president-elect trusted.

As General Scott mentally ran through the list of possibilities, one name stood out: Senator William H. Seward of New York.

Seward was known as a friendly colleague and staunch supporter of the new president. Lincoln had already asked for his advice on several issues, and the senator would soon join the new president's cabinet as secretary of state.

Clearly, Seward was the man for the job.

But it was now ten a.m. Only forty-eight hours were left before Lincoln reached Baltimore. If Senator Seward was going to warn the president-elect in time, he had to move.

Quickly, Scott penned a message to Seward and told Colonel Stone to deliver it.

At the Capitol Building, Stone handed Scott's note to the New York senator and briefed him on all the morning's events. Seward listened carefully. Like many others, he had worried about possible assassination attempts, and Stone's report confirmed what he had feared all along. It was vital to warn Lincoln immediately. But, again, the question was: Who would do it? Seward himself couldn't leave Washington at the moment—but he knew of someone who could.

After asking Colonel Stone to write down a complete summary of the facts in Bookstaver's report, the senator sent out a call for his thirty-year-old son. Luckily, as it turned out, Frederick Seward was only a few steps away. The young man, a journalist, was sitting in the Senate chamber. He was busy covering the proceedings for his newspaper, when a page "touched [him] on the elbow" and asked him to meet his father in the lobby. There, the older Seward handed Frederick the note from General Scott and a letter the senator had just written to Lincoln. Then, in a low voice, he explained the situation.

"General Scott is impressed with the belief that the danger is real," Seward told his son. "Colonel Stone . . . is not apt to exaggerate. I want you to go by the first train. Find Mr. Lincoln, wherever he is. Let no one know your errand [and tell him that] I think he should change his arrangements and pass through Baltimore at a different time."

Pausing only to grab his coat, Frederick Seward charged out of the Capitol, rushed to the station, and caught the first train to Philadelphia. By now it was early afternoon. The hours were ticking away. But—if the train was on time—young Seward would catch up with the president-elect that very evening.

Chapter 19

"I FULLY APPRECIATE THESE SUGGESTIONS."

Philadelphia, Pennsylvania
Morning to eleven p.m., February 21, 1861

Frederick Seward's train was chugging north, but Allan Pinkerton had already reached Philadelphia.

The detective had decided that the only way to avoid trouble in Baltimore was to completely change all the president-elect's travel plans. Instead of letting Lincoln arrive on the afternoon of Saturday, February 23, as scheduled, Pinkerton had decided to fool the conspirators by sneaking the new president through Baltimore thirty-six hours before he was expected. To do it, Lincoln would have to leave Philadelphia secretly this very night on the eleven p.m. train. He would slip through Baltimore about four hours later and arrive in Washington the following morning—February 22—a whole day earlier than planned.

The idea was simple. Arranging to carry it out was not.

First, the detective had to meet with Samuel Felton, the head of the Philadelphia, Wilmington, and Baltimore Railroad. Since Pinkerton was hoping to put Lincoln and a small security escort into one of the PW&B Railroad's sleeping cars that very night, Felton's cooperation was essential. This, however, was no issue. Felton, after all, had originally hired Pinkerton. He wanted to protect both his railroad and the new president, so he instantly promised to do anything that would ensure Lincoln's safety.

That took care of the first item on Pinkerton's list. But even more important than securing Felton's cooperation was talking to Norman Judd.

Before the detective could take another step, he had to fully brief Judd on the situation in Baltimore and explain his plan to alter Lincoln's travel arrangements. He had to wait for Lincoln's trusted advisor to explain those facts to the president-elect. And he had to hope that Lincoln would agree to the plan.

Clearly, nothing could happen without the help of

Norman Judd. So Pinkerton instructed his assistant George Burns to give Lincoln's advisor a note specifying the time and place of a meeting as soon as the president-elect's party reached Philadelphia.

By now the groundwork was in place. Most of the preparations had been made, and there was nothing to do but wait for Judd's arrival. But Judd was traveling with the new president, and the *Lincoln Special* was taking a slow, roundabout route to Philadelphia.

That morning the president-elect had traveled from New York to New Jersey by ferry. Then he had boarded a train that would carry him to Trenton, New Jersey's capital city. But although the actual journey had gone smoothly, it had not been a particularly pleasant one. Most New Jersey residents hadn't voted for Lincoln. Few came out to cheer for the president-elect, and—as he rode through Newark—Lincoln saw a large doll dressed to look like him hanging from a lamppost with a noose around its neck. It was another ugly reminder of the fact that almost half the country hated the new president and wished him dead.

Still, the day wasn't completely depressing. In the New Jersey State House legislators cheered when Mr. Lincoln said, "I shall do all that may be in my power to promote a peaceful settlement of all our difficulties." And when the *Lincoln Special* finally roared into Philadelphia at four p.m., the whole city turned out to celebrate.

There were cannon salutes, marching bands, and a pushing, shoving, crazy "wild mass of human beings" craning their necks to get a look at the new president.

From his seat beside Lincoln in the president-elect's carriage, Norman Judd was watching the cheering crowd when a man suddenly forced his way through a line of policemen, dodged around the cavalry company that was protecting the new president, and dashed straight toward him.

For a moment it looked like the stranger was going to attack Mr. Lincoln. But this time the man was not an assassin. He was Pinkerton's assistant George Burns, carrying out his orders. As he trotted along beside the carriage, Burns thrust a note into Judd's hand. He waited while the president-elect's advisor read it, and he heard Judd agree to meet Pinkerton at the St. Louis Hotel as soon as possible.

But the new president's advisor didn't exactly hurry.

Two hours later, at six o'clock, Pinkerton was still waiting. The clock was ticking. And Mr. Judd hadn't shown up.

The train that would carry Mr. Lincoln to Baltimore was scheduled to leave at eleven. But the detective couldn't put Lincoln on board without Judd's help. So where on earth was the new president's advisor?

In New York, Kate Warne had told Judd that the

situation was critical. She had explained that meeting Pinkerton in Philadelphia was essential. And Judd knew that the president-elect's life was in danger. But at six thirty he still hadn't reached Pinkerton's hotel. And all the frustrated detective could do was wait—until Judd finally walked through the door at six forty-five.

In a rush, Pinkerton updated Judd on the plot. He explained his plan to sneak the president-elect through Baltimore. He emphasized the danger, and he pointed out that the train would leave soon. Speed was now essential. Lincoln's consent had to be obtained immediately. It was time for the president-elect's advisor to act.

But Norman Judd just nodded . . . and sat.

Yes, Mr. Judd agreed, the threat did seem serious. And yes, Pinkerton's plan to sneak Lincoln through Baltimore was certainly good. But that didn't matter—because the president-elect probably wouldn't agree to go through with it.

For months now, Mr. Lincoln had refused to accept the fact that some people wanted him dead. The threats, he thought, were nonsense. The danger, he said, was imaginary. And at this point, he wasn't likely to change his mind.

Still, Judd pointed out, Lincoln knew Pinkerton. For years he'd respected the detective's judgment. So maybe if Pinkerton talked to him directly, if the detective personally presented the facts, the new president might just listen.

But there was a problem. It was nine p.m., and the train would leave at eleven. That left only two hours—two short hours to meet the president-elect, convince him of the danger, and get him to the station.

Together, Judd and Pinkerton set out to find Lincoln. But the streets were packed. The sidewalks were clogged. Movement was almost impossible, and so many people were jammed in front of the president-elect's hotel that Pinkerton and Judd couldn't squeeze through the front door. Desperate and determined, the two men fought their way through the vast, heaving mob and finally slipped into the hotel through a staff entrance.

But inside was no better. The lobby and stairs were swarming with visitors. In one room Mr. Lincoln was walled in by a crowd of admirers. There was no possible way to attract his attention, so—as a last resort—Judd handed one of Lincoln's secretaries a note saying that he needed to see the president-elect urgently. He ordered the man to deliver it. And as Judd and Pinkerton waited, the clock ticked.

Nine fifteen turned into nine thirty.

Nine thirty became ten.

One after another the minutes passed. The situation seemed hopeless. The plan couldn't possibly work. But then, at ten fifteen, Mr. Lincoln walked into Judd's room.

With only forty-five minutes left before train time, Pinkerton swiftly laid out the facts. He told the president-elect about Ferrandini. He explained the conspirators' vicious plan to attack at the Baltimore railroad station. And he spoke of the dangerous mood in Maryland. It was a scary description that might have frightened many men, but Lincoln showed no sign of panic. Everything about him was "cool, calm, and collected," as—in a lawyerly way—he cross-examined the detective on every point. The evidence appeared to add up, and—reluctantly—Mr. Lincoln agreed. The threat did seem to be serious.

Allan Pinkerton had made his case.

Now, it was up to Judd.

In a few terse sentences, the president-elect's advisor outlined the plan to sneak Lincoln through Baltimore. It was a good idea, he conceded. It might well save the new president's life. But, Judd pointed out, it could also be a public relations disaster.

The problem, he said, was that vengeful members of Ferrandini's gang might murder Pinkerton and Harry Davies if those agents ever publicly described how they had learned the names of the conspirators and uncovered the plot. This meant that proof of the serious threat in Baltimore could never be revealed to the nation. And without proof that the president-elect had actually been in danger, people might call Lincoln a coward. They might say that he'd sneaked through Baltimore just because he was too chicken to appear in a hostile, pro-secessionist, slaveholding city. "If you follow the course suggested . . . ," and travel to Washington right now, Mr. Judd told the president-elect, "you will . . . be subjected to the scoffs and sneers of your enemies, and the disapproval of your friends who cannot be made to believe in the existence of so desperate a plot." The choice, Judd concluded, was between safety and bad publicity. Still, the decision was Lincoln's. And it took the new president only seconds to make up his mind.

"I fully appreciate these suggestions . . . ," Mr. Lincoln said courteously. "But I cannot go to-night." The next day, the president-elect explained, he had a full schedule that included a flag-raising ceremony, speeches, a visit to Independence Hall (where the Constitution and the Declaration of Independence had been adopted), and official meetings in Pennsylvania's capital city, Harrisburg. But if Pinkerton and Judd could put together a plan that would allow him to keep all his engagements and still get through Baltimore ahead of schedule, he would consider it in the morning. Then—and only then—would he make a final decision on the matter. But for now, the president-elect had had enough. It had been a long day. The hour was late, and he was ready for sleep.

But as Mr. Lincoln neared his bedroom, he saw that the light was on.

The door was open.

And a stranger was standing near the doorway.

Frederick Seward, son of Senator William H. Seward.
He was sent by his father to warn Abraham Lincoln about the Baltimore plot.

Chapter 20

"I SHALL THINK IT OVER CAREFULLY."

Philadelphia, Pennsylvania
Ten p.m. to midnight, February 21, 1861

The stranger could have been Ferrandini. It could have been Hillard. It could have been any one of the Baltimore conspirators. But, in fact, it was Frederick Seward—harried, rumpled—and relieved to be meeting Mr. Lincoln at last.

All day Senator Seward's son had been trying to carry out his father's orders. All day he'd been trying to give the president-elect his father's warning about an assassination plot. And nothing about that day had been easy.

The long train ride from Washington had been

"tedious." The locomotive hadn't pulled into Philadelphia until ten p.m., and then young Seward had had to push his way through the crowded streets to Lincoln's hotel.

Inside he found the "brilliantly-lighted" rooms packed with ladies and gentlemen. Everyone seemed to be shaking hands with the new president, and Seward instantly realized that this was not the time or the place to deliver his urgent message to Mr. Lincoln. But he couldn't just give up and go home. Somehow, he had to get to the president-elect—and he had to do it soon.

As the young man tried to think of a reasonable plan, he saw Lincoln's son Robert standing nearby. Robert was likely to know how to contact his famous father, so Seward walked up and introduced himself. The two chatted briefly. Robert, however, couldn't offer any immediate help. But he did present Seward to Colonel Ward Hill Lamon, one of Lincoln's oldest friends and advisors.

Lamon, eager to do anything he could for Senator Seward's son, offered to take the young man in to see Lincoln immediately. But when Seward explained that his message was personal and confidential, the colonel understood.

In that case, Lamon said, "I think I had better take you to his bedroom. If you don't mind waiting there, you'll be sure to meet him . . . and it is the only place I know of where he will be likely to be alone." It was a perfect solution, and after thanking the colonel, Seward settled down in the president-elect's room.

At about eleven p.m. footsteps sounded, and the young man saw Lincoln coming down the hall. Lamon introduced Seward to the new president, and Seward—who had never before seen Mr. Lincoln in person—was immediately struck by the president-elect's "pleasant, kindly smile."

After chatting with the young man for a few moments about affairs in Washington, Mr. Lincoln got down to business. He sat down at a lamplit table, opened Senator Seward's letter, and reviewed the information that General Scott and Colonel Stone had compiled about a possible assassination plot in Baltimore.

As Senator Seward's son watched, Lincoln read the pages once. He read them twice. He looked up, paused for a moment, and then began to pepper the young man with questions.

Did young Seward know anything about how General Scott and Colonel Stone had learned about this plot?

No. Seward had no idea.

Could the information possibly have come from a detective named Allan Pinkerton?

No. Seward had never heard the name Pinkerton mentioned.

Again, Mr. Lincoln paused. "I may as well tell you why I ask," he said. "There were stories or rumors . . . before

I left home, about people who were intending to do me a mischief. I never attached much importance to them— never wanted to believe any such thing. So I never would do anything . . . in the way of taking precautions. . . . Some of my friends, though . . . without my knowledge employed a detective [named Pinkerton] to look into the matter . . . and to-day he . . . [brought me a story similar to yours] about an attempt on my life in . . . Baltimore."

Well, Seward replied, it seemed that Pinkerton's information confirmed the report he'd brought from General Scott and Colonel Stone.

But Mr. Lincoln smiled and shook his head. "That is exactly why I was asking you about names," he said. "If [two] different . . . [detectives] not knowing of each other's work [have independently come up with the same information]," then one report would confirm the other. But "if this is only the same story" from the same source being told by two different people, it provides no additional proof.

It was a sensible conclusion, and Seward couldn't argue with Lincoln's logic. Still, the young man pointed out, there was a good chance that the investigations had been conducted separately and that the danger was real. So why take a chance? Surely, Seward said, it made sense to change the travel schedule in order to avoid any possible risk.

For a few more minutes the men discussed the situation,

and then Mr. Lincoln rose. "Well," he said, "we haven't got to decide it to-night, any way, and I see it is getting late." Nonetheless, the new president added, "I shall think it over carefully . . . and I will let you know in the morning."

There was nothing left to say. Seward had done his best. He'd delivered his message. He'd warned Lincoln of the danger. He'd begged the president-elect to take precautions. But only Lincoln could make the final decision, and Seward could only wait to see what the new president would decide.

PASSENGER AND FREIGHT STATIONS, PRESIDENT STREET, BALTIMORE.

Baltimore's President Street Station, where assassins
planned to carry out the attack against Abraham Lincoln.

Chapter 21

SO WHAT COULD GO WRONG?

Philadelphia, Pennsylvania
Midnight to four thirty a.m., February 22, 1861

It was midnight, but Allan Pinkerton was still wide-awake. Mr. Lincoln's refusal to immediately head south had upset the detective's first plan, but Pinkerton was now determined to come up with a scheme that would allow the president-elect to make all his Pennsylvania political appearances and still get safely through Baltimore ahead of schedule. But fitting one more thing into Lincoln's busy official program was going to be a challenge.

On February 22, the new president's day would start

at six in the morning when he was scheduled to make a speech and raise a flag at Philadelphia's Independence Hall. Between nine thirty a.m. and one thirty p.m. he would be traveling from Philadelphia to Harrisburg by train. After that, he was supposed to make a speech to the Pennsylvania General Assembly and dine with the governor of Pennsylvania at five p.m. Then, and only then, would Mr. Lincoln be free to travel south—if Pinkerton could make the arrangements.

The problem was difficult but not impossible, and gradually, the detective began to put together a plan. It was a good plan. But he couldn't carry it out single-handed. So, as most Philadelphians snoozed on their pillows, Pinkerton began to assemble a team.

First, the detective sped through the Philadelphia's dark, deserted streets to visit George Franciscus, a loyal Lincoln man and an important executive with the Pennsylvania Railroad. Despite the hour, Franciscus was still hard at work in his office. He willingly listened to the detective's proposal, agreed to help, and accompanied Pinkerton back to Norman Judd's hotel room.

By that time Judd had been joined by another key player: Henry Sanford. Sanford, a man whose devotion to Lincoln was unquestioned, was a communications expert who worked for the American Telegraph Company. Each of the four was committed to helping the president-elect, and together they began to map out a plan that would ensure Lincoln's safety.

Multiple issues had to be discussed, and the first was the question of railway connections. Although trains ran regularly from Philadelphia to Baltimore, there was no direct rail link between Baltimore and Harrisburg. This meant that the first problem was finding a way to secretly transport Lincoln from Harrisburg to Philadelphia so that he could slip aboard the eleven p.m. Baltimore-bound express.

Not surprisingly, it was railroad man George Franciscus who came up with a solution. He offered to provide a special Pennsylvania Railroad train for Lincoln's private use. It would be a small train, made up of only a locomotive, a passenger car, and a baggage car, but it would leave Harrisburg at about six p.m. and arrive at the West Philadelphia railroad station at about ten thirty.

Pinkerton, who would be waiting at the West Philadelphia depot with a carriage, would then escort Mr. Lincoln across town to the Philadelphia, Wilmington, and Baltimore railroad station. Then both men would sneak aboard a sleeping car on the southbound eleven p.m. train.

Baltimore, however, was the last stop on the PW&B Railroad line, and Lincoln still had to go on to Washington. So when the express reached Baltimore at about three thirty a.m., the sleeping car—with Pinkerton and Lincoln in it—

would be detached from the Philadelphia, Wilmington, and Baltimore train. Then it would be dragged across town by a team of horses to another railroad station, where it would be attached to a Baltimore and Ohio Railroad train that would get Lincoln to the capital by about six in the morning.

During the trip, Lincoln would have to be disguised. He would have to be smuggled in and out of trains and railroad stations without being recognized. He would have to be accompanied by one or more bodyguards at all times—and none of this would be simple.

For hours the men discussed the details. The plan was big. It was complicated. But it seemed possible.

So what could go wrong?

The answer was: everything.

Back in the early stages of the investigation, Pinkerton had learned that the conspirators had a code for sending information about Lincoln's movements along the telegraph lines. He was aware that Ferrandini might now have spies watching the president-elect, and he knew that such a spy might get wind of the plan and telegraph the news of Lincoln's change in travel plans to Baltimore. If that happened, Ferrandini and the other conspirators could alter their tactics. They could easily launch an early, unexpected attack on Lincoln. And the result could be disaster. It was up to Pinkerton and his colleagues to prevent that kind of security breach. They had to ensure secrecy, but it was hard to know how.

This time, however, Henry Sanford, the American Telegraph Company's representative, thought of a way. The best solution, Mr. Sanford said, was to cut the telegraph lines between Harrisburg and Baltimore as soon as Lincoln set out. That way no dangerous messages could pass between those cities during the president-elect's journey, and the lines could easily be repaired as soon as Mr. Lincoln reached Washington.

It was the last part of the puzzle. The details had all been ironed out, and at four thirty a.m., the meeting broke up. In the next few hours, Franciscus would arrange for the special train. Sanford would instruct a couple of trusted men to take care of the telegraph lines. Judd would present the plan to the president-elect, while Pinkerton would coordinate all the elements and get ready to act as Lincoln's bodyguard during the most dangerous part of the journey.

In the predawn darkness, the men went their separate ways. During the last hours, they had done their best to ensure that the new president would reach Washington safely. But although the plan seemed good, it still had one basic flaw— Mr. Lincoln hadn't yet agreed to go through with it.

At one of the many celebrations during his journey to Washington,
Abraham Lincoln raises a flag outside Independence Hall in
Philadelphia, Pennsylvania, to celebrate George Washington's birthday.

Chapter 22

"ONE OF THE THOUSAND THREATS AGAINST YOU"

Philadelphia and Harrisburg, Pennsylvania;
Baltimore, Maryland
Six a.m. to afternoon, February 22, 1861

It was a cold, gray morning, but at six a.m. Lincoln was already up, dressed, and on his way, the Philadelphia's Independence Hall with little Tad beside him. As four white horses pulled his carriage up to the entry, Mr. Lincoln could see that a crowd of almost thirty thousand people had come to see him celebrate the birthday of the first U.S. president, George Washington, by raising a flag at the birthplace of the American nation.

At the door, dignitaries greeted Mr. Lincoln and then escorted him inside to the room where the Declaration of Independence had been signed.

With his hat in his hand, the president-elect looked around. He saw the wide windows. He saw the elegant paneling. He looked at the carved decorations. But it wasn't the beauty of the room that interested him—it was the fact that in 1776, fifty-six men gathered in that room had risked their lives by signing a document that:

—freed the thirteen American colonies from England,

—boldly declared that "all men are created equal,"

—and stated that all people are entitled to the "unalienable" rights of "Life, Liberty, and the pursuit of Happiness."

Onlookers noted that Mr. Lincoln seemed deeply moved. And when the president-elect spoke, it was clear he believed that the principles of liberty and equality expressed in the Declaration were the true foundation of America. "I have never had a feeling, politically," he said, "that did not spring from the sentiments embodied in the Declaration of Independence." The Declaration, Lincoln noted, "gave liberty, not alone to the people of this country, but I hope to the world for all future time. . . ." But, he added, the Declaration of Independence did something more. It also made a promise. It promised "that in due time [freedom would be given to] all men." Indeed, said the new president, the principles expressed in the Declaration of Independence were so basic, so fundamental, and so important to the nation, that, "I would rather be assassinated on this spot than surrender [them]."

It was a moving, heartfelt speech, but listeners had little time to absorb the president-elect's important words. A brightening light showed that the morning sun was rising, and it was time to get on with the ceremony.

Outside, people applauded as Mr. Lincoln stepped forward, took off his coat, and hauled on the flagpole ropes until the Stars and Stripes shot up into the breeze. As the Union flag with its thirty-four stars streamed out, the crowd cheered. A band played "The Star-Spangled Banner," and many waved little flags of their own. For a moment it seemed as if the crowd could only think of their love for America. For a moment it seemed that they had set aside their fears of secession, their fears of war, and their fear of the hatred that half the country felt for the new president.

But Allan Pinkerton hadn't forgotten about any of those things.

So while thirty thousand people cheered for Lincoln and the flag, the detective was doing his best to save the new president. At an early-morning meeting Pinkerton had already issued instructions to his assistant George

Dunn. Dunn was to quickly head for the railway station and buy sleeping-car tickets on the eleven p.m. southbound Philadelphia, Wilmington, and Baltimore train for Lincoln and three companions. Once he had the tickets, Pinkerton's assistant was to give them to Agent Kate Warne, who had recently come to Philadelphia to help her boss. Mrs. Warne would then go to the station at night. There, she would use the tickets to reserve four berths in the rear of the train's sleeping car. Then she would escort the president-elect's party to those berths—*if* they arrived at the station.

If, if, if, if. The word must have been driving Pinkerton crazy. Hours had now passed since his evening meeting with the new president, but the detective still didn't know *if* Lincoln had agreed to carry out his plan. Finding out had become a necessity. So at eight a.m. Pinkerton knocked on the door of Mr. Judd's hotel room.

But the room was empty.

Norman Judd was with the president-elect, and Mr. Lincoln was introducing his longtime advisor to young Frederick Seward. Seward, the president-elect told Judd, had just been "sent by his father [Senator Seward] to inform me of the same conspiracy that you and Pinkerton explained to me last night. . . ." And, added Lincoln, he also "advises that I proceed immediately to Washington." Now, Judd, said the president-elect, turning to his advisor, "You can explain to him . . . what has been done."

Judd, of course, did not want to reveal the details of Pinkerton's plan, but he told the young man that arrangements were being made to get Lincoln to Washington safely. Having done that, the president-elect's advisor left his boss, returned to his own hotel room—and found Pinkerton waiting.

The night before, Norman Judd had argued that having Lincoln sneak through Baltimore would be a public relations disaster. Now, however, he had changed his mind. Though still worried about the publicity issue, Judd now felt that Pinkerton's plan was the best way to protect the new president. The problem was that Lincoln had still not decided if he was going to change his travel program. So, to keep all their options open, the two men mapped out a plan. While Judd awaited the president-elect's final decision, Pinkerton would make all the necessary arrangements for the secret trip. That way everything would be ready to go—*if* and when Mr. Lincoln gave the word.

With that settled, the two men separated. Judd had to join Lincoln on the nine thirty a.m. train to Harrisburg and discuss the Baltimore trip with the new president. Pinkerton needed to work out some last-minute details. But while Judd and Pinkerton were carrying out their individual programs, a nameless woman walked down a Baltimore street, entered a post office, and mailed a letter to Mr. Abraham Lincoln. It read:

Dear Sir

I think it is my duty to inform you that I was advised last night by a gentleman that there existed in Baltimore, a league of ten persons, who had sworn that you should never pass through this city alive—This may be but one of the thousand threats against you that have emanated from some paltry Southerners, but you should know it . . . (so) your friends may be watchful. . . . God defend you and bless you—The prayers of many go with you.
A Lady

It was another terrible reminder that the threat against the president-elect's life was real.

Chapter 23

THE MOB WANTS BLOOD

New York City; Baltimore, Maryland; Washington, D.C.
Seven a.m. to late afternoon, February 22, 1861

For American politicians, February 22 was a busy travel day—and Abraham Lincoln wasn't the only important person using the railways.

At seven o'clock that morning U.S. Vice President–Elect Hannibal Hamlin and his wife, Ellen, left New York City. They crossed the Hudson River to New Jersey and headed on to Philadelphia, where they planned to pick up a noon train that would carry them through Baltimore and on to Washington.

No one, apparently, had made a special effort to warn

Hamlin about possible danger in Baltimore, but the new vice president was a cautious man. For years, as a U.S. congressman and senator, he'd fought so hard to abolish slavery that one South Carolina newspaper claimed—falsely—that Hamlin was part African American. With his record, the vice president–elect knew he'd be hated in pro-slavery, pro-secession Baltimore. He knew the city had a history of violence, and he was so concerned about being attacked that he'd considered leaving his young wife safely at home in Maine. Friends had convinced him that he could get both himself and Mrs. Hamlin to Washington in one piece, but the new vice president still felt he should take precautions.

When making his travel arrangements, Hamlin had asked Mr. Samuel Felton, president of the Philadelphia, Wilmington, and Baltimore Railroad, to attach a special sleeping car to the PW&B train that would carry the vice president–elect and his wife through Maryland. Felton, of course, agreed, and the idea definitely made sense. With the nation's attention focused on Lincoln, no one was paying much attention to the vice president. Few knew where he was on any given day. So if Hamlin and his wife made their entire journey south hidden in curtained berths in a darkened sleeping car, there was a good chance that they would slip through Baltimore without ever being noticed.

Certainly, everything looked good at noon when

the new vice president and his wife quietly boarded the sleeping car on their southbound train. They traveled through Pennsylvania and down into Delaware with no major incidents. But there was no point in being careless. And both Mr. and Mrs. Hamlin were safely tucked in their dark sleeping berths with the curtains drawn as the train rumbled into the Baltimore station.

Outside there were noises—the clank of the train wheels, the squeal of the brakes. Then, suddenly, Hamlin and his wife heard angry voices. There was a bang. The sleeping-car door was wrenched open, and a drunken crowd of toughs forced their way inside. Someone had told the mob that the vice president–elect was on the train, and now the attackers seemed to want blood. Screaming that "no damned Abolitionist like Lincoln or Hamlin should enter the White House," they roared through the car, ripping open curtains and looking for Hamlin. For one long, terrifying moment the gang stared at the new vice president and his wife in their berths.

But Hamlin's face was not well-known. None of the ruffians recognized him, and finally the thugs left almost as abruptly as they had come.

With the shaken vice president–elect and his wife still inside, their sleeping car was detached from the locomotive, hitched to a team of horses, and safely dragged across town to another railroad station. There, it was attached to a Washington-bound train, and a few hours later Mr. and Mrs. Hamlin stepped out of their car onto the streets of the nation's capital.

By sheer chance, the new vice president and his wife had made it through Baltimore alive. But no one knew if Mr. Lincoln would be that lucky.

Chapter 24

"WHAT IS YOUR OWN JUDGMENT UPON THIS MATTER?"

Harrisburg, Pennsylvania
One thirty p.m. to six p.m., February 22, 1861

For Abraham Lincoln, it was another long, exhausting day. First, there had been the flag raising and the train trip from Philadelphia to Harrisburg. Then he'd appeared on the balcony of a Harrisburg hotel to assure a rowdy crowd that he wanted to "preserve the peace of this country so far as it can possibly be done. . . ." After that he'd had to shake hands, travel to the state capitol building, and make yet another speech. So it was late in the afternoon when the president-elect was finally able to gather all his advisors in a hotel room for a briefing on the possible assassination threat in Maryland.

As the Lincoln staff listened, Judd described the possible danger and explained how Pinkerton had uncovered the Baltimore plot. He pointed out that the detective's findings had been independently confirmed by Frederick Seward. And he detailed Pinkerton's plan to secretly sneak the president-elect through Baltimore on that evening's train.

Horrified and surprised, the men struggled to grasp this terrible news. Then, like a bunch of overheated volcanoes, they erupted with questions. Was the danger Judd had described real? Was it severe enough to justify this secret trip? Did Pinkerton's plan have flaws? Would the action help or hurt the new president? Opinions and ideas flew back and forth. One elderly army officer loudly declared that the whole idea of sneaking the president-elect through Baltimore was a "d—d piece of cowardice." Lincoln, he thought, should just fight his way through the city at the head of a cavalry division. Others, however, worried that jokers would make fun of the new president for dodging the pro-secession city. But some argued that saving Mr. Lincoln's life was so important that all possible risks should be avoided.

Back and forth the discussion went until, finally, Judge David Davis, a senior staff member, turned to the president-elect. "Well, Mr. Lincoln, "he said, "what is your own judgment upon this matter?"

By this time the new president had had most of the day to weigh the evidence and consider the pros and cons of avoiding Baltimore. He'd listened to his advisors' opinions. He may even have recalled that an important northern newspaper editor had once said to him, "[Mr. Lincoln,] your life is not safe, and it is your simple duty to be very careful."

The time for argument was now past. A decision had to be made, and the president-elect was ready to make it.

In a calm, level voice he said, "I have thought over this matter considerably since . . . last night. The appearance of Mr. Frederick Seward, with warning from another source, confirms my belief in Mr. Pinkerton's statement. Unless there are some other reasons, besides fear of ridicule, I am disposed to carry out . . . [Pinkerton's] plan."

"Well," said Judge Davis, "that settles the matter. . . ."

And it did—mostly. But before the meeting ended, there was one other question that the group had to resolve: Who would act as Lincoln's bodyguard during the first part of the trip?

On the surface, it seemed logical to give the job to one of the president-elect's military advisors. But—at about age sixty—Colonel Edwin Sumner was too old. Colonel Ellsworth might be recognized from the drawings of him that had appeared in the papers. And Major David Hunter couldn't use one arm because he was suffering from a dislocated shoulder. So, who should it be?

To Judd, the answer was obvious. The man Lincoln needed was sitting right there in that hotel room. He was one of Lincoln's closest friends, and his name was Ward Hill Lamon.

Tall, broad, and strong, Lamon was a mountain of a man who went everywhere armed with a knife, two pistols, and a blackjack. Traveling with him would be like traveling with a human tank. Just the sight of this big bearded man bristling with weapons would probably scare off most attackers, and Lamon was willing to take on the assignment.

But it was getting late. If the plan was going to work, Lincoln had to leave for Philadelphia shortly, and the president-elect's wife still hadn't been told about the threat or the change in her husband's travel schedule.

Did Mr. Lincoln break the news to her himself? Did he ask Norman Judd—a man Mrs. Lincoln distrusted— to do it for him? Or did both of them tell her about the situation? No one knows for sure, but it's very clear that the new president's wife didn't like what she heard and that she said so—loudly, angrily, and forcefully.

Back in Springfield, Mrs. Lincoln had seen some of the threatening letters her husband received. She knew he'd had an eerie vision of his own death, and she realized that an assassination attempt could be made at any time. Still, she had sworn to stay by her husband's side, "danger or no danger." And now it seemed she was determined to keep that promise. Furious at the idea of being separated from her adored husband at the very moment when he might need her, she began to shout out her feelings.

Fearing that Mrs. Lincoln's angry cries might accidentally reveal details of Pinkerton's travel plan, the president-elect's staff panicked. Instead of trying to calm and console the upset woman, they locked the sobbing Mrs. Lincoln in her hotel room. Then they concentrated on getting her husband ready for his five o'clock dinner with the governor of Pennsylvania.

For a while the new president and the governor chatted at the table, but at five forty-five, Mr. Lincoln rose from his chair. After saying that he felt tired, the president-elect left the party and went up to his room to prepare for the journey.

The first big problem, he knew, was getting out of the hotel without being recognized. In the past months hundreds of newspapers had published colorful descriptions of his tall, thin, lanky body. Pictures of his distinctive face had been plastered on thousands of campaign buttons and banners. Almost everybody in America's thirty-four states had a pretty good idea of what the new president looked like; but now, somehow, he had to conceal his identity.

In his hotel room, Mr. Lincoln rummaged through his luggage, looking for a disguise. He put on an old overcoat over his usual black suit. He picked up a shawl that could be used to hide the lower part of his face. But he needed something more to cover his head. Almost everyone knew that he always wore a tall black stovepipe hat, so that wouldn't do. But sitting in his baggage was another hat—the flat-crowned, soft, wide-brimmed hat that he'd been given in New York City. Never in his life had the president-elect worn such headgear, and no one would expect him to wear such a thing now. The soft hat was perfect.

Overcoat, hat, shawl . . . he was almost ready. But there was one thing he still needed. If he made it to Washington alive, he would have to deliver his inauguration speech at the swearing-in ceremony. That speech—that important, top secret speech that outlined his true thoughts about America's current problems—had made the journey from Springfield to Pennsylvania in his old black satchel. For most of the trip Mr. Lincoln had personally carried that bag from place to place. For most of the journey he'd kept it close beside him—and he wasn't likely to leave it behind now.

Disguised and ready, the president-elect left his room. He made his way through the halls and down the staircase. There were people about, but nobody paid much attention to the tall, striding man in an old overcoat. He continued on—past the lobby, out the door—and within minutes, Lincoln and his bodyguard, Lamon, were in a carriage on their way to the railroad station.

At the depot, as planned, a special train was waiting. Although the beam of the locomotive's headlamp shone out brightly into the night, there were no lights in the passenger car. Darkness was essential to make sure that no one saw Mr. Lincoln's face through the windows.

Inside, the president-elect and Lamon settled into their seats and stared out into the blackness. Up front, in the locomotive, the train crew had already received their instructions. They were to travel fast, make no unnecessary stops, and arrive in Philadelphia promptly at ten p.m.

The schedule was tight, and there was no room for delays. It was time to get started. In the cab, the engineer pulled on the throttle. The wheels turned. The train jerked forward. It picked up speed—and, as it rushed along the track, a technician cut the telegraph lines between Harrisburg and Baltimore. For the next few hours, no telegraph messages could travel between those two cities. During that time, no enemy spy in Harrisburg could alert the Maryland conspirators to Mr. Lincoln's change of travel plans. No Harrisburg journalist could tell the country that the new president had mysteriously disappeared from Pennsylvania's capital city. And no would-be assassin would know exactly where to find Mr. Lincoln.

So far everything had gone according to plan. But a million other things could still go wrong. And as the president-elect's train sped through darkness, everyone on the Lincoln/Pinkerton team knew that the next twelve hours would be crucial.

Chapter 25

"WHERE IS NUTS?"

Philadelphia, Pennsylvania
Six thirty p.m. to eleven p.m., February 22, 1861

It was now well past six o'clock, and in Philadelphia, Allan Pinkerton was practically exploding with questions. Had the president left his Harrisburg hotel safely? Was he on the train? Had the locomotive left the Harrisburg station? The detective had made sure that one telegraph line from Harrisburg to Philadelphia would be left open so that he could communicate with his assistants. But at seven o'clock, he had no word. At eight the telegraph wires were still silent, and by eight thirty he clearly couldn't stand the suspense another minute.

Using a previously agreed on code name for the president-elect, Pinkerton sent a brief telegram to his Harrisburg agent. It read:

Where is Nuts (Lincoln)?

Eight forty-five came.

Nine.

And still no answer. Had something gone wrong? Had Lincoln been delayed? The minutes were trickling by like frozen molasses. What on earth could be taking this long? Then, abruptly—as the clock hands pointed to nine fifteen—the telegraph clattered. Dah-dit. Dit-dit-dah. Dah. Dit-dit-dit. . . . Finally. A message:

Nuts left at six—Everything as you directed—all is right.

It was the signal Pinkerton had been waiting for. Mr. Lincoln was on his way, and it was time for the detective to get busy.

First, he picked up Kate Warne at her hotel, put her in a carriage, and sent her off to the Philadelphia, Wilmington, and Baltimore depot. There, she was to reserve sleeping-car berths for the president-elect's party on the eleven p.m. southbound train and wait for the arrival of the travelers.

With that done, Pinkerton swiftly hired another coach. Then he ordered the driver to take him to another Philadelphia railway station, where he would meet

Mr. Lincoln's Harrisburg train.

It was still early when the detective reached the depot. The train wasn't yet due, so Pinkerton waited outside with the carriage. But not for long. The Harrisburg locomotive crew had obeyed their travel instructions to the letter. They'd been told to get to Philadelphia by ten. And at three minutes past the hour—much earlier than he'd expected—the detective saw Lincoln and Lamon coming toward him. Quickly, before anyone could recognize the president-elect, he hustled the new arrivals into the waiting coach and slammed the door.

But now there was a problem. The Baltimore train was scheduled to leave at eleven. The trip across town from one railway depot to the other would take only a few minutes. And that left almost an hour, an hour during which Pinkerton had to make sure that no one—no murderer, reporter, or admirer—could identify Mr. Lincoln or reveal his unexpected presence in Philadelphia. Somehow, for the next hour, the detective had to hide the new president. But where?

To Pinkerton, the answer was obvious. Because no one could see a face through the windows of a moving roofed coach in the nighttime darkness, the safest place for Mr. Lincoln was inside the carriage. So, before climbing into the coach, Pinkerton ordered the driver to take a roundabout route through the city and deliver them to the Philadelphia,

Wilmington, and Baltimore station in an hour's time.

Safety, of course, was on everyone's mind. As the coach rolled through the Philadelphia streets, Lamon asked if Lincoln personally wanted to carry a pistol or knife for protection; but the detective immediately objected. People might laugh if the new president arrived in Washington looking like weapon-toting gunslinger. And Pinkerton didn't want that to happen. With luck, there would be no trouble and no violence. But, said the detective, "if fighting had to be done, it must be done by others." Not the president-elect. Mr. Lincoln firmly agreed. In his usual calm, precise way, the new president pointed out that he wasn't afraid. He didn't want to carry knives or pistols. And besides, he was quite sure that Pinkerton's plan "would work right."

For almost an hour, the men talked and circled the city. But while they were discussing possible problems, Kate Warne was facing a real one. At the Philadelphia, Wilmington, and Baltimore depot, she was having trouble reserving four sleeping berths next to one another on the eleven p.m. southbound train.

Although sleeping-berth reservations could usually be made, some unknown person had decided that, on this particular train, bunks would be handed out on a first-come, first-served basis. And that was a problem for two reasons. First, if other passengers crowded in, there was a chance that no bunks would be left for the late-arriving presidential party. Furthermore, on a crowded train, it might not be possible to secure four berths together—and that meant that Lincoln's guards might not be near enough to protect the president-elect during the journey.

It was an annoying, unexpected difficulty. But if Agent Warne was annoyed or upset, she didn't show it. Instead, she pulled money out of her purse, slipped the conductor a fat tip, and persuaded him to hold four berths for her poor, dear, sick brother and his three companions.

That took care of the sleeping-car arrangements, but the Pinkerton agents had more to do before the new president arrived. While Mrs. Warne stood guard over the reserved berths, one of Pinkerton's other assistants, George Dunn, began to check out the rest of the train's passengers. And he didn't like what he saw.

Standing at the front of the sleeping car were a bunch of shady-looking characters. They might be troublemakers— or they might not. Dunn didn't really know. Still, there was no point in taking chances. To avoid the toughs, Pinkerton's assistant decided to arrange for the Lincoln party to enter the sleeper through the back door. But someone had locked the rear entrance. Only the porter could open it, and it took Dunn several anxious minutes to persuade the man to give him the key.

By now it was almost eleven. The train was just about

ready to leave. As the last passengers were boarding, Mrs. Warne spied three men moving along the platform. Lincoln—in his soft hat, shawl, and overcoat—was stooping down, holding Lamon's arm, and trying to look like an invalid. But his disguise didn't fool the Pinkerton agent. She instantly recognized the party. Rushing forward, she greeted Mr. Lincoln as if he were really her poor, dear, very sick brother. Then she efficiently escorted the travelers to their berths.

In the dimly lit car, the president-elect's party tried to settle themselves in their bunks. Lincoln was so tall that he couldn't completely stretch out in his, but Warne, Pinkerton, and Lamon were presumably tucked up in their berths when a sharp blast from the whistle split the air. Wheels clanked. A plume of smoke shot from the engine, and within minutes the train was steaming out of the Philadelphia station. It was heading south and taking Abraham Lincoln—a man known for his opposition to slavery—into hostile slave territory.

Once again, almost everything had gone according to plan. But now Lincoln, Lamon, Pinkerton, and Warne were facing the most perilous part of their journey. And as the train hurtled through the night, none of them knew what to expect in Baltimore.

Chapter 26

DREAD AND DANGER

Philadelphia, Pennsylvania;
Baltimore, Maryland
Eleven p.m. to four thirty a.m.,
February 22–23, 1861

Some passengers on the president-elect's train may have slept that night, but Allan Pinkerton probably never closed his eyes. As yet, there was no sign that news of Lincoln's secret journey had leaked out, but the detective knew a security breach was possible. Alert and undoubtedly nervous, Pinkerton prowled the sleeping car, watching for trouble. Back and forth he went, keeping an eye on the passengers and occasionally ducking out on the rear platform to check for possible hazards along the track.

Since there were some places along the route where the train could be easily ambushed, bombed, or derailed, the detective had stationed agents near those spots to watch for suspicious activity. Each had been instructed to raise a lantern as the train passed to tell Pinkerton that it was safe to go ahead. Now, one after another, the lights flashed in the darkness. So far, so good. But still, the detective must have worried. There was always a chance that one of his agents had been fooled or had missed a clue. And Pinkerton must have been tense as the train approached one of the journey's most dangerous spots: the mile-wide Susquehanna River crossing.

Because there was no bridge here, the president-elect's train would have to be rolled onto a steamboat, ferried across to the other side, and then put back on the track. At any time during this long, tedious process, assassins could invade the cars, blow up the train, or even sink the steamer. So the detective was on guard and ready for trouble as the ferry left the port and made its way across the river. The trip was slow. For the travelers, it must have been nerve-wracking. But then—suddenly—it was over. The steamer had tied up at the dock, and they were safe—safe on the opposite shore. The first crisis point was past, and— for a moment—Pinkerton could breathe a little easier. Even the extraordinarily calm president-elect seemed a bit relieved. "We are getting along quite well," he said cheerfully, as the train started up again.

And Mr. Lincoln was right. So far—almost everything had gone according to plan. But now they were in Maryland—a state where the president-elect was hated, where slavery was popular, and where many supported secession. There was no telling what would happen here, and every member of the Lincoln party was wide-awake when the train finally clanged into Baltimore's President Street Station at around three thirty a.m.

For Kate Warne, it was the last stop. There was business Pinkerton wanted her to take care of in Baltimore, so the detective escorted her off the train and then returned to guard Lincoln.

As they waited at the station, things seemed fairly quiet. But—because the president-elect now had to change trains in this unfriendly city—Allan Pinkerton knew that the next hour would be the most dangerous of the entire trip.

In Baltimore, railway workers had to detach the new president's sleeping car from the PW&B train, hitch it to a team of horses, drive a mile across town to another railroad station, and then attach the car to a Washington-bound Baltimore and Ohio Railroad locomotive. With luck, the whole process would happen in the predawn darkness, go smoothly, and take about forty-five minutes. But the detective knew that any number of things could go wrong.

- An unexpected delay in the process could leave Mr. Lincoln stranded in the hostile city for hours.
- A Baltimore mobster might recognize the president-elect and start a riot.
- And if, by some horrible chance, the conspirators had gotten wind of Mr. Lincoln's secret trip, they might attack at the next station or while the sleeping car was being dragged through the city.

Nothing was certain. But as the wary detective peered out of the rolling railway car during the crosstown trip, he saw only the dark, deserted streets of Baltimore, and he heard only the steady clip-clop of hooves in the early-morning silence. So far everything had gone smoothly, but Pinkerton didn't dare relax. An attack might come at any moment. A sudden threat might erupt in the darkness. So the detective kept a sharp eye out as the railroad horses pulled Lincoln's sleeping car down President Street, along Pratt Street, past the waterfront, and—finally—into the city's Camden Street Railroad Station. Another crisis point was past.

Then, suddenly, there was a problem.

To avoid trouble, the president-elect had to get out of Baltimore as quickly as possible—but there was a delay at the Camden Street depot. The Washington-bound locomotive scheduled to haul Lincoln's car into the capital was running late. Nobody knew when it would arrive. The new president might now be stuck in this dangerous Maryland city for hours. And, to make matters worse, the detective spied some suspicious characters milling around the station platform.

Still, the danger and delay didn't seem to bother Mr. Lincoln. To kill time, he told jokes in a hushed voice and seemed to be "as full of fun as ever." But the detective was only too well aware that the strange man who was hitting the railroad ticket agent's booth with a club might decide to use his stick on Mr. Lincoln. And he also knew that the drunk singing "Dixie" could easily be a secessionist rebel who wanted to kill the president-elect.

Inside the train, the men waited while the drinker roared out verse after verse of one of the South's most popular songs:

> *I wish I was in the land of cotton,*
> *Old times there are not forgotten;*
> *Look away! Look away! Look away! Dixie Land.*
>
> *. . . I wish I was in Dixie, hooray! Hooray!*
> *In Dixie's Land I'll take my stand*
> *To live and die in Dixie. . . .*

It was a rollicking melody, but at the moment, the words didn't make the president-elect's party feel very cheerful. Instead, those lyrics seemed to be another grim reminder of the great national divide and the possibility of war between the North and the South. To Pinkerton, it seemed that the new president recognized this. When Mr. Lincoln commented, "No doubt there will be a great time in Dixie by and by," the detective thought he sounded sad.

But now time was passing. The Washington train still hadn't arrived. Soon it would be dawn, and daylight would increase the chance that some enemy would recognize the president-elect.

The clock was steadily ticking, and every moment was bringing them closer to sunrise.

Would the engine ever come?

And then there was a sound. It was the sound of wheels rattling along a railway track. The tardy locomotive had arrived at last.

Railroad workers joined the cars, and soon the president-elect's train was moving out of the station. It was picking up speed and flying through the countryside.

Now there were only thirty-eight miles left in the journey, and soon—very soon—the president's party would be in Washington. After a long, hard night of dread and danger, they were almost there.

Chapter 27

"HIGHLY IMPORTANT NEWS"

Washington, D.C.; Baltimore, Maryland
February 23-March 3, 1861

The sun was just starting to come up when the early-morning train from Baltimore pulled into Washington. The worst was over, but Pinkerton remained on edge as he watched the tired Lincoln party step out onto the station platform.

Lincoln, still dressed in his soft hat, overcoat, and shawl, looked more like a "well-to-do" small-town "farmer" than his usual self. But his odd costume didn't fool his old friend, Congressman Elihu Washburne, who happened to be waiting at the station. As the disguised president-elect walked by, Washburne called out, "Abe, you can't play that [trick] on me." Then the congressman stretched out an arm to give Mr. Lincoln a welcoming handshake. It was a casual, friendly gesture. But to the exhausted, overstressed Pinkerton, it looked like an attack. Determined to protect Lincoln at all costs, the detective immediately sent Washburne staggering with a sharp elbow punch. He was moving in to deliver a second blow when the president-elect seized Pinkerton's arm. "Don't strike him Allan, don't strike him," Lincoln called out. "That is my old friend Washburne. . . ." Somewhat grudgingly, the detective apologized. Washburne politely accepted, and together the four men drove off to Willard's Hotel where Mr. Lincoln would be staying until the inauguration.

By now, the new president must have wanted a wash and a rest. But since the hotel manager hadn't expected Lincoln to arrive so early, his room wasn't ready. It was an unfortunate situation, but the president-elect made the best of it. After first asking the hotel manager if he could borrow some slippers, Lincoln had breakfast with Senator Seward, got ready to call on various Washington officials, and sent a telegram to his wife saying that he had made the trip safely.

Learning that her husband was unharmed was probably the best thing that had happened to Mary Lincoln in the past twenty-four hours, but she didn't have much time to enjoy her feeling of relief. In Harrisburg the remaining members of the Lincoln team were packing up, and in a little while, Mrs. Lincoln, the children, and most of the new president's advisors had to board a train that would take them from Harrisburg, to Baltimore, and then on to Washington.

Since newspapers had not yet broken the story of Lincoln's secret trip, the Baltimore assassins were still expecting the president-elect and his family to arrive on the afternoon train. But what would Ferrandini and his crew do when they discovered that the new president was not among the passengers? Would they turn their rage on Mrs. Lincoln? Or would they refuse to attack an innocent woman and her children? None of Lincoln's advisors knew, but it was clear that there might be trouble.

And there was.

When Mrs. Lincoln's train pulled into the Baltimore depot, a huge, ugly mob armed with stones and rotten eggs surged toward the cars. Still unaware that the president-elect was not aboard, some people screamed curses. Others howled, "Trot him out," "Let's have him," "Come out, Old Abe," "We'll give you hell." One man who looked a little like the new president was almost injured, and there was a good chance that Ferrandini and his murderous friends were lurking in the crowd. If Lincoln had been on board, he might well have been killed or hurt. But he wasn't, and neither was his family.

According to most accounts, Mrs. Lincoln and the boys got off the train shortly before the cars pulled into the Baltimore station. While the mob yelled its disappointment at not finding the president-elect, the Lincoln family lunched quietly with friends. Later, they were driven safely across town to pick up the Washington-bound train and arrived in the capital without further problems.

So far it had been a busy Saturday—and the day wasn't yet over.

While Mrs. Lincoln was traveling and Mr. Lincoln was meeting with officials in Washington, frantic reporters were trying to piece together the story of Lincoln's secret trip to the capital. But it wasn't until Monday morning that readers of *The New York Times* saw a headline that read:

HIGHLY IMPORTANT NEWS

Secret Departure of the President Elect from Harrisburgh

Alleged Plot for His Assassination

UNEXPECTED ARRIVAL IN WASHINGTON

Surprise of the Harrisburgh People, and Indignation of the Baltimoreans

Soon every paper in the country had picked up the story, and people were arguing passionately about whether Mr. Lincoln had done the right thing. *The New York Times* strongly felt that the president-elect's decision had been correct. Not surprisingly, *The Baltimore Sun* disagreed. Lincoln, they said, had behaved like a "lunatic." In Cleveland, *The Plain Dealer* scolded the new president for acting like a coward and said he was "wanting in pluck." Readers of *The New York Herald* were told that Abraham Lincoln had behaved more like a "thief in the night" than a U.S. president, and political cartoonists had a field day.

Since *The New York Times* had reported—incorrectly— that Lincoln had been disguised in a Scottish plaid cap and a long cape, artists drew pictures of the tall, long-legged president-elect dancing in a Scottish kilt or muffled to the eyebrows in a cloak with a silly plaid cap on his head.

The cartoons were funny, and—as Judd had predicted— some people did laugh at Lincoln. Others were angry because they felt the president-elect had made a stupid decision. But no one was more upset than the Baltimore conspirators. During a meeting with Pinkerton, James Luckett swore that Ferrandini had had "twenty picked men with good revolvers and Knives" in the crowd. They would have, he said, "murdered the d—d Abolitionist had it not been that they were cheated." But, Luckett added, Ferrandini and the others weren't going to give up. They would simply "make . . . [another] attempt to assassinate Lincoln." Still, it would clearly take some time for the assassins to regroup, and at the moment, it seemed no definite plans for a second try had been made.

In Baltimore, Pinkerton and his agents continued to monitor the situation. But in Washington, Mr. Lincoln had already put the incident behind him. Later he would tell a friend, "I did not then, nor do I now believe I should have been assassinated had I gone through Baltimore as first contemplated, but I thought it wise to run no risk where no risk was necessary." In any case, the decision had been made. The deed had been done, and Mr. Lincoln had more important things to worry about. The presidential inauguration was now only nine days away. And in nine days, on March 4, Mr. Lincoln was finally going to tell Americans how he truly felt about secession and war when he delivered his inaugural address.

Before leaving Springfield, he'd spent days writing his speech. For weeks he'd refused to tell the public exactly what it was going to say. But now it was time. It was time to reveal his secret thoughts. It was time to open his little black satchel, take out his speech, and tell the entire country how he planned to handle the national crisis.

Mr. Lincoln believed, of course, that the basic ideas behind his speech were sound, but the words and tone had to be perfect. In each and every sentence he had to explain his thoughts clearly. He had to make people understand where he stood on the issues. He had to tell Americans how he would deal with the secession problem. And he had to show the country that he would be a fair, firm, and prudent leader.

It was a tall order.

So in the days before the inauguration, Mr. Lincoln carefully reread his speech. To get some idea of how his ideas might be received, the president-elect asked his colleague Senator Seward to review the text. Then, after considering Seward's comments, Abraham Lincoln sat down, picked up a pen, and began to edit his words.

The inauguration of Abraham Lincoln at the U.S. Capitol, 1861.

Chapter 28

THE PRESIDENT SPEAKS

Washington, D.C.
Inauguration Day, March 4, 1861

It was Inauguration Day—the day America had been waiting for. Citizens everywhere were hoping that the new president would finally reveal his thoughts about the national crisis, and the whole country was wondering what he would say.

In New York City, huge crowds gathered outside newspaper offices so they could read the very first printed copies of Lincoln's inaugural address. At their headquarters in St. Joseph, Missouri, Pony Express riders stood ready to carry news of the speech across two thousand miles of mountains, prairies, and deserts to Sacramento, California. Washington hotels were crammed with visitors, and over thirty thousand people were streaming toward the Capitol Building so they could hear the new president's words in person. Police and soldiers patrolled the streets, while up on the rooftops armed sharpshooters stood ready to protect Mr. Lincoln from possible assassins.

At Willard's Hotel, the new president had been up since five. The night before, he'd spent a good deal of time reviewing and editing his speech. To make sure that his points were clear, that the sentences flowed, and that the words would sound right to an audience, he'd listened carefully as his son Robert read the paragraphs aloud. But another rehearsal couldn't hurt, so in the morning Mr. Lincoln practiced again by delivering the speech to his wife and children. Then, with that done, the new president sat alone for a while, waiting for the ceremonies to begin.

At noon, he made his way downstairs dressed in a new black suit, wearing a shiny black stovepipe hat, and holding a fancy gold-headed cane. Within minutes outgoing president James Buchanan arrived. A band struck up "Hail to the Chief." And as the two men walked out to a waiting carriage, they made a strange pair—with the tall, thin, middle-aged Lincoln towering over the short, plump, white-haired, old Buchanan. People cheered, flags fluttered, trumpets blared, and slowly the two drove together down Pennsylvania Avenue until they reached the Capitol.

The great dome that now crowns the Capitol Building was still under construction, but a platform had been erected at the top of the stairs in front of the columned entryway. In the center, a small table had been set up; and at the sides, on benches, sat senators, members of the House of Representatives, Supreme Court justices, and other dignitaries. Senator Edward Baker, a good friend of Mr. Lincoln's, delivered a short speech introducing the new president, and then Lincoln came forward.

Taking the pages of his speech from his pocket, he anchored them firmly on the table with his cane, and then hesitated. For a moment, he seemed unsure of where to put his hat. But, sensing the new president's dilemma, an old political rival stepped in. Senator Stephen Douglas had furiously debated Lincoln in the past. He'd beaten Abraham Lincoln in an election for the U.S. Senate and had been beaten by Lincoln in the 1860 presidential election. But at the moment those bygone contests seemed to be forgotten. With a gracious gesture, the senator picked up the president's stovepipe, set it carefully on his own lap, and held it securely during the rest of the ceremony.

Now, as the spectators settled down, all eyes turned toward Mr. Lincoln. With his spectacles on his nose and the manuscript of his speech in front of him, the new president began to speak. His voice was light and "high-pitched," but his words carried clearly to the distant edges of the crowd.

First, like the lawyer he was, Mr. Lincoln talked about the basic law of the land, the Constitution. It was important, he explained, for everyone to understand just how the laws in that important document affected the nation's quarrel over secession and slavery.

Now, said the president, it was clear that "one section of our country believes slavery is right . . . while the other believes it is wrong." But both the North and the South needed to realize that—as it was then written—the Constitution did not give him or any other U.S. president the "lawful right" to personally and immediately abolish slavery.

On the other hand, Mr. Lincoln pointed out, the Constitution also did not give the southern states the legal right to secede. The union of states, he said, was "perpetual." "No state, upon its own mere motion, can lawfully get out of the Union," said the president, and any state that tried was committing a crime.

So, would he start a war to bring back these criminal, runaway, seceded southern states? No. There would be no fighting, Mr. Lincoln promised, unless the South fired the first shot. But, he said, the South had to remember one very important point. By swearing the presidential oath, he was swearing to "preserve, protect, and defend" the nation. That meant he had a "most solemn" duty to hold on to all U.S. property and to fight back if the seceded southern states dared to attack the people, possessions, or government of the United States.

Still, Mr. Lincoln said, *he did not want war.* "We are not enemies," he told Americans, "but friends. We must not be enemies. . . ." And this argument must not "break our bonds of affection." Instead of harping on differences, the president said, both northerners and southerners should remember the "mystic cords"—the shared memories, the shared patriotism, and the shared beliefs—that forever bound Americans together. Then, with that in mind, both sides should work to resolve their problems lawfully, sensibly, and honorably—as if touched by "the better angels of our nature."

As the sound of Mr. Lincoln's last words died away, the chief justice of the Supreme Court stepped up to administer the presidential oath of office. With his big hand resting on the Bible, Abraham Lincoln repeated the words that every American president since George Washington had said: "I do solemnly swear that I will faithfully execute the Office of President of the United States, and will, to the best of my Ability, preserve, protect, and defend the Constitution of the United States."

And that was that. By saying those words, Mr. Lincoln

had promised to do everything he could to keep the whole country together.

The ceremony was over. Abraham Lincoln was now officially president. But as some in the crowd cheered and "hurrahed," others were already starting to argue about the inaugural speech.

In the Confederate South, many denounced Lincoln's speech as a blunt "declaration of war."

To Black abolitionist Frederick Douglass, the speech was a bitter disappointment. Because Lincoln seemed to think that saving the Union was more important than wiping out, "the foul withering curse of slavery," Douglass felt that the new president had betrayed African Americans and the abolitionist cause.

In the North, Lincoln's supporters said the president's words were, "strong, straightforward and manly." But Lincoln's northern opponents called the address a "rambling . . . loose-jointed" rant that was meant to start a war. One southern woman groused that the speech was just like the new U.S. president, "stupid, ambiguous, vulgar, and insolent." And, of course, there were lots of northerners and southerners who simply thought the speech was weak, muddled, and unclear and showed that Lincoln still hadn't made up his mind about the issues.

Back and forth the arguments went. But despite the complaints of his critics, Abraham Lincoln's words were not weak. They were not stupid, and they were not muddled. In his inaugural address, the president had carefully and deliberately made two clear and important promises: He had promised not to go to war unless the South fired the first shot, and he had promised that he would fight to defend land, property, people, and government of the United States from Confederate attack.

So, as he shook hands with admirers after the ceremony and later escorted his beautifully gowned wife to a grand inaugural ball, Abraham Lincoln knew exactly what he had said to the nation. He knew he had made two significant promises. But Mr. Lincoln also knew that making promises was easy.

The hard part was keeping them.

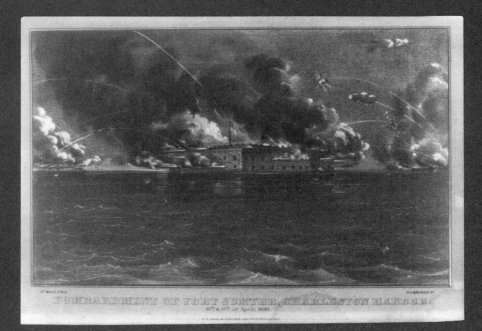

A print showing the Confederate bombardment of Fort Sumter.

Chapter 29

"IF THIS MUST BE DONE, *I* MUST DO IT."

Washington, D.C.; South Carolina; Montgomery, Alabama
March 5-April 17, 1861

It was early—so early that some of the previous night's inaugural ball guests may still have been in their beds. But Mr. Lincoln was up, in his office, and busy. The Baltimore crisis was past, and the ceremonies were over. Now, it was time for the president to get down to business, and the first item on his to-do list was an urgent dispatch from Major Robert Anderson, the military commander at U.S. Fort Sumter.

The letter was short and straightforward. It said that

the sixty-eight soldiers stationed at Sumter were running out of supplies. At the moment they had barely enough food, medicine, and ammunition to last another six weeks. The situation was serious, and they needed immediate assistance.

To many people, that would have sounded like a simple, ordinary request.

But to Abraham Lincoln, it was a screaming, flashing red-light signal of danger.

Fort Sumter, the president knew, wasn't just any U.S. stronghold. This island fort was located in southern waters about three miles off the coast of South Carolina in the very heart of the Confederacy. The shores around Sumter bristled with Confederate guns and cannons. Five thousand Confederate troops were stationed nearby, and many southerners were longing to capture this important U.S. outpost.

To bring supplies to Sumter, U.S. navy ships would have to sail into a section of the sea that was part of Confederate territory. And that was a problem. It was a problem because if U.S. warships actually entered those waters, the Confederate government could claim that the United States was invading the South.

To protect their homeland and stop the "invasion," Confederate troops would undoubtedly fire on the U.S. ships. Then the South would say that the United States government had started a war by sending U.S. military attack forces into Confederate territory.

But if Lincoln didn't send supplies to Sumter, Major Anderson and his starving troops would be forced to leave the fort. Confederate forces would then seize Sumter, and a valuable piece of U.S. property would fall into enemy hands.

So, what should the president do?

Just the day before, in his inauguration speech, Mr. Lincoln had made two promises to the American people. He had promised not to start a war, and he had promised to "preserve, protect, and defend" all U.S. property. Then, saying those words had been easy. But now nothing was simple. If the president resupplied Sumter—if he ordered U.S. navy supply ships to sail into southern territory—he would probably start a war. But if he didn't send supplies, he would violate his presidential oath by letting an important piece of U.S. property fall into the hands of the rebel Confederate states. If Lincoln kept one promise, it looked like he would have to break the other.

The danger was clear, and the choices were awful. The president had to decide. But he didn't have to make that decision in a hurry. Since Major Anderson and his troops still had six weeks' worth of supplies, Mr. Lincoln had time—time to think about the problem and time to discuss a strategy with his advisors.

A few days later, when his new cabinet officers came to the White House for a meeting, Lincoln briefed them on the crisis. As the restless president paced the room, his advisors talked about possible options. But there was only one basic question: Should the United States send supplies to Sumter? Since the answer was crucial, the president asked each man to present his opinion in writing. Then he tallied the responses.

Postmaster-General Montgomery Blair said yes. Supplies should be sent to Sumter because it was important to "maintain the authority of the [U.S.] Government."

Four other cabinet officers—Secretary of State William Seward, Secretary of War Simon Cameron, Secretary of the Navy Gideon Welles, and Secretary of the Interior Caleb Smith—said no. Sending supplies to Sumter, they argued, would certainly start a war.

And the treasury secretary, Salmon Chase, was undecided.

The cabinet couldn't agree, but the decision wasn't up to them. Only the president could make the final choice, and Mr. Lincoln knew it. "If this must be done, *I* must do it," he told his secretary of state. But the truth was he didn't know what to do, and every day the situation was becoming more serious.

By March 28 the kitchen storeroom at Fort Sumter held only one barrel of flour, a little pork, a few carrots, and a bit of rice. Major Anderson's soldiers were facing starvation. They couldn't hold out much longer, and Mr. Lincoln had to do something.

Of course, he didn't want Sumter to fall into Confederate hands. Like many others, he realized that the U.S. might eventually have to fight to restore the Union and solve the problem of slavery. But war was a terrible thing. It would plunge America into a long agony of death and destruction, and Abraham Lincoln—a man who personally hated violence—did not want to condemn his nation to bloodshed and suffering.

Each day the president carried on with his normal public rounds. He signed official papers. He consulted with advisors. He shook hands and met distinguished visitors. At a dinner party he made guests laugh with an endless stream of jokes and funny stories. But in private, the problem preyed on his mind and his emotions. At night he wrapped himself in an old bathrobe and sat alone, unable to sleep. During the day, he admitted he was sometimes "in the dumps." And on March 30 stress brought on a migraine headache so severe that Mr. Lincoln "keeled over." Later the president would tell a friend, "Of all the trials I have had since I came [to the White House], none begins to compare with those I [suffered over Sumter]. They were so great that could I have anticipated them, I would not have believed it possible to survive them."

But it wasn't only the Sumter decision that weighed on his mind and heart. In those early spring days, nothing seemed to go right. In Washington, rain poured down incessantly from gloomy skies. At the White House, Willie and Tad came down with measles—a serious disease that often killed children in the days before modern scientists learned to prevent it with vaccination. And, to top it all off, the newspapers got wind of the Sumter crisis and began to criticize the president.

"Wanted—A Policy," cried the April 3 *New York Times.* If Mr. Lincoln doesn't make a decision soon, said the paper, "The Union will not only be severed, but the country will be disgraced." Opponents argued that the nation's only hope was to immediately overthrow the president and his "demoralizing, disorganizing, destructive" party. Even a loyal supporter told Lincoln that most Americans felt that almost anything was better than "this uncertain state of things."

But the days passed, and still Lincoln hesitated.

At Sumter supplies were running out faster than expected. But when Major Anderson asked Washington when he should abandon the fort, he received no clear instructions.

Advisors made suggestions. Possibilities were considered. More days drifted by. Then—almost at the last minute—the president had an idea.

What if he sent only food—but no guns or ammunition—
to Fort Sumter?

If the rescue ships carried only food and no military
supplies, surely the Confederates would understand that
this was an aid mission—not an attempt to attack the
South. Southerners would have no reason to fire on a
bunch of hunger relief ships. And maybe—just maybe—he
could get supplies to Sumter without starting a war. It was
a chance—a long chance—but it was worth taking.

On April 6, Mr. Lincoln sent a message to the
Confederate government saying that the United States
was going to "supply Fort Sumter with provisions
only. . . ." And, the president added, if southerners did not
attack the food ships, the United States would make no
further attempt to supply Sumter with "men, arms, or
ammunition." It was a reasonable offer, but no one knew
if Jefferson Davis would agree.

In his Montgomery, Alabama, office, the new
Confederate president and his cabinet officers met to
discuss the problem. But from the start, Davis's views
were clear. He was dead set against letting Lincoln send
food to Sumter. Instead, he wanted to seize the fort. And,
said Mr. Davis, if Anderson's force didn't leave voluntarily,
he thought the southern army should immediately bomb
the U.S. troops out of Sumter.

War was what the Confederate president wanted.

War was what most of his cabinet officers favored. But Confederate Secretary of State Robert Toombs objected.

Firing on Sumter, said Toombs, would be "suicide." If the South attacked that fort, he told the Confederate president, it would start "a civil war greater than any the world has yet seen." It would, Toombs said, stir up a vast nest of northern "hornets" who "will swarm out and sting [the South] to death."

It was good advice, but Jefferson Davis was a stubborn, stiff-necked man. For weeks he'd been predicting war, and now he seemed determined to make his own predictions come true. Instead of negotiating, delaying, or even considering Toombs's counsel, he directed General P. G. T. Beauregard, commander of the southern troops surrounding Sumter, to seize the fort.

On April 11—before Lincoln's food ships had even reached South Carolina—the general sent a note to Major Anderson. It read, "I am ordered by the Government of the Confederate States to demand the evacuation of Fort Sumter. . . ."

But Anderson refused. In a polite dispatch, he explained that his duty to the U.S. government made giving up the fort impossible.

It was a standoff.

Major Anderson couldn't give in.

The Confederate government wouldn't.

And on April 12, 1861, at four thirty a.m., southern guns began to bombard Fort Sumter.

For thirty-three hours Confederate cannons blazed. For almost a day and a half they blasted the U.S. stronghold. And on April 13, with no food in their bellies and the fort almost in ruins, Major Anderson and his men were forced to surrender. Defeated but still proud, U.S. forces left Sumter the following day—flying the U.S. flag they had bravely defended.

Five hundred miles away, in Washington D.C., Abraham Lincoln heard the news. The waiting was over. The choice had been made, and the president had kept his first promise. He had not started a war. The South had done that. By firing on Fort Sumter, the Confederacy had attacked the United States. And now—to keep his second promise—Mr. Lincoln moved swiftly to defend his nation.

On April 15 he sent out a call for seventy-five thousand troops. "Loyal citizens" from all over the North came forward to protect "the honor, integrity, and the existence of [the] National Union." And among those volunteers was Allan Pinkerton. Abolitionist, Union supporter, and a loyal Lincoln man, the detective promptly sent the president a letter offering to carry out top secret wartime spy missions for the U.S. government.

In the South, Jefferson Davis also asked for army volunteers. Eager Confederate recruits swore that they could beat the "cowardly" Yankee "rascals" one-handed. And southerners celebrated when the states of Virginia, North Carolina, Tennessee, and Arkansas seceded and joined the Confederacy.

The break between the North and the South was now complete. After simmering for over two hundred years, American's long quarrel over slavery had finally exploded into civil war. And for those who still hoped that the United States would survive, there was only one question: Could Abraham Lincoln save the nation?

Frederick Douglass, an escaped slave who became an abolitionist, rights activist, powerful orator, newspaper owner, and author. He spoke and consulted with President Lincoln about slavery, recruiting Black soldiers, and allowing Black people to vote.

Chapter 30

"FOREVER FREE"

Washington, D.C.
April 1861–April 1865

The war was long, bloody, and terrible. Some thought it was fought only to save the Union, but Abraham Lincoln knew better. He believed that slavery, not secession, was the true cause of this dreadful conflict. To him, the Civil War was God's way of punishing America for the sin of enslaving Black people. It was a war he feared would go on until "every drop of blood drawn by the [slave owners'] lash shall be paid by another drawn by the sword." And he realized that the country could never be reunited unless America solved the problem of slavery.

Back in 1858, before he was elected, Mr. Lincoln had told Americans that the nation could not continue to exist "half-*slave* and half-*free*." It had to become, he explained, "*all* one thing, or *all* the other." And there was no place for slavery in a country that, the president said, was "conceived in Liberty, and dedicated to the proposition that all men are created equal." To save the country, Lincoln had to eliminate this terrible evil. And Frederick Douglass, the great Black abolitionist and newspaper editor, was one of the people who encouraged the president to do it.

To Lincoln, Douglass was "one of the most meritorious men in America." To Douglass, the president was a man who received him as "one gentleman receives another," talked to him "freely," and did not let him "feel for a moment that there was any difference in the color of our skins." In their meetings, the two men got on well. They respected each other. They both hated slavery. But Douglass, a former slave, wanted the president to end slavery immediately. And Lincoln, a political realist, knew that was impossible—because many Americans were not yet ready to liberate slaves.

Even in the mostly anti-slavery North, some people feared that two different races could not live peaceably in freedom together. Some northern voters were opposed to ending slavery, while others thought that the country might not be able cope with a sudden flood of four million newly freed slaves who had no money, no homes, and—for the most part—little education. If Lincoln moved too fast, there was a chance that these anti-abolition voters might decide to throw the president and his party out of office and elect pro-slavery officials instead.

But coping with fear and prejudice wasn't the only problem President Lincoln faced. He also had to deal with the fact that not all the slave states had seceded.

Four slave states on the southern border—Delaware, Maryland, Kentucky, and Missouri—had stayed in the Union. And though some of their citizens objected, those states were doing a lot to help the United States fight the South. If Lincoln tried to abolish slavery immediately, those border states might decide to leave the Union and join the Confederacy. That, of course, would make it much harder for the North to win the war. And if the North didn't win, there was no hope of getting rid of slavery.

So, what could the president do?

How could he overcome these obstacles?

Sometimes, at night, when he sat alone and sleepless in the White House library, Lincoln must have tried to find an answer. But there was no easy solution. There was no way to solve the problem all at once. So he began with baby steps.

First, Mr. Lincoln approved a new federal law saying that runaway slaves could not be returned to their rebel

Confederate masters. Then, he signed another law that abolished slavery in the nation's capital, Washington, D.C. But when the president suggested that the U.S. government pay slave owners in the border states to free their slaves, those slave owners objected. They flatly refused to take part in the program.

And Mr. Lincoln couldn't force them.

He couldn't order loyal citizens of the United States to give up their legally owned slaves. The Constitution didn't give him that right, and the president had to obey the Constitution. For a while it seemed that the fight against slavery had stalled. But then Abraham Lincoln had an idea.

As a lawyer, he knew that the Constitution didn't give him the power to force loyal U.S. citizens to give up their slaves, but the slave owners in the Confederate states *weren't* loyal U.S. citizens. They were rebels. They were enemies fighting a war against the United States— and that was an important point. It was important because one of Mr. Lincoln's jobs as president was serving as the commander in chief of all U.S. armed forces. As commander in chief he *did* have the constitutional power to attack all U.S. foes. And one way to attack both slavery and the nation's Confederate enemies was for Mr. Lincoln to use his power as commander in chief to issue an order that freed all Confederate slaves.

Now, of course, the president knew that giving liberty to slaves in the Confederacy wouldn't end all slavery, but it was a place to start. Before issuing the order, Lincoln carefully considered his decision. He consulted his cabinet. He spent several months drafting the document that we now call the Emancipation Proclamation. And on New Year's Day 1863, Mr. Lincoln signed his new Proclamation into law. It read: "I, Abraham Lincoln, President of the United States of America and Commander-in-chief of the Army and Navy thereof, do hereby proclaim and declare that . . . on the first day of January in the year of our Lord, one thousand eight hundred and sixty-three, all persons held as slaves [in the rebel states] shall be then, thenceforward, and forever free. . . ."

The words were fancy, but the meaning was clear. In simple terms the Emancipation Proclamation declared that under U.S. law all slaves in the Confederacy were now free to leave their masters. It said that the U.S. government was now committed to protecting the freedom of those liberated slaves. And it was the biggest, boldest step anyone had ever taken to end slavery in America.

In northern cities African Americans celebrated, sang, and prayed. In Boston, Pittsburgh, Chicago, and Buffalo joyful citizens—both Black and white—fired hundred-gun salutes. Frederick Douglass celebrated by writing in his newspaper, "We shout for joy that we live to record this righteous decree." And as he prepared to sign the Proclamation, Mr. Lincoln said, "I never in my life, felt more certain that I was doing right, than I do in signing this paper. If my name goes into history it will be for this act, and my whole soul is in it."

But, of course, not everyone was happy. In the slave state of Kentucky, the furious governor wanted his legislature to completely "reject the emancipation Proclamation." To the governor of New York, Lincoln's act was a "bloody, barbarous, revolutionary, and unconstitutional scheme." Some Union soldiers dropped their guns and left the northern army because they didn't want to fight for Black freedom. A group of Midwest Democrats threatened to make peace with the Confederacy and kick Lincoln and his "abolitionist faction" out of office. Race riots broke out in some cities. Some angry whites called Lincoln a "tyrant," and the uproar frightened some members of Lincoln's own Republican party so much that they begged the president to withdraw the Proclamation. But Lincoln refused. "My word is out to these people," he said, "and I can't take it back."

He was convinced that slavery had to be destroyed. As time went on, many more U.S. citizens began to agree with him. And when Abraham Lincoln ran for reelection in 1864, a majority of northern voters showed their support for his anti-slavery policy by electing him to a second term as president.

Now, with most voters behind him and signs showing that the North was likely to win the war, Mr. Lincoln pushed ahead.

Issuing the Emancipation Proclamation had been a good start, but that document had only freed the slaves in rebel states. The next step was to completely outlaw slavery in all parts of the country. And to do that, Americans had to amend—change—the Constitution so that it abolished slavery forever.

But changing the Constitution was a hard, complicated process. First, two-thirds of the U.S. Senate and the U.S. House of Representatives had to agree to add the amendment—the change—to the Constitution. Then, three-quarters of the states had to approve it. Mr. Lincoln knew that getting that many people to agree to anything would be difficult, but the job had to be done.

Using every tactic he knew, the president pushed Congress into voting for the new Thirteenth Amendment to the Constitution. He pressed. He persuaded. He encouraged. He reminded members that slavery was "the greatest wrong inflicted on any people." He told them that the country had to protect "the millions now in bondage [and the] unborn millions to come." This amendment had to pass, he said.

And it did. First, the Senate agreed to the measure. Then, on January 31, 1865, the House of Representatives adopted it. By the end of March 1865, nineteen states had ratified—approved—the change, and more were considering it. But before any of those other states could act, the war suddenly ended.

On April 9, 1865, in the parlor of a red brick house in the little village of Appomattox Court House, Virginia, Confederate general in chief Robert E. Lee surrendered to the chief officer of the northern army, Lieutenant General Ulysses S. Grant. The Confederate rebellion was over. The federal Union had been saved. And—with the new Thirteenth Amendment—the United States was in the process of putting an end to slavery. But the cost had been terrible. Somewhere between six hundred thousand and seven hundred fifty thousand people—more than in any other American war—had died in the conflict. Billions had been spent. Countless tears had been shed. Much of the South stood in ruins, and angry southerners now wished that all Yankees would "land in the seventh hell and blister forever." But in cities across the North people sang in the streets. Businesses closed for celebrations, and in Detroit a flyer proclaimed the general feeling. "The Year of Jubilee has come! Let all the People rejoice!" it read.

At the White House, the president seemed like a new man. Without the stress and sorrow of war, he was so happy that Mrs. Lincoln said, "Dear Husband, you almost startle me by your great cheerfulness." Yes, the president replied, "and well may I feel so. . . ." The battle was over. He had accomplished what he set out to do, and now—after years of almost forgetting how to laugh and feeling he might "never be glad again"—he was determined to be "more cheerful in the future."

But while the president and Mrs. Lincoln shared their happiness, a twenty-six-year-old actor named John Wilkes Booth was brooding over the end of slavery and the Confederate defeat. Born in a Baltimore suburb, Booth always claimed that his "soul, life, and possessions are for the South." Like many nineteenth-century southerners, he felt that America was "formed for the *white*, not for the *black* man." And now he believed that he personally had to do something "decisive and great" to punish Lincoln for ending slavery and destroying the old southern way of life.

In the spring of 1865, as Union armies marched toward their final victory, Booth and a group of angry southern sympathizers began to make plans to kidnap or murder the president. For weeks they plotted in Washington bars and boardinghouses. And in those weeks, an alert detective might have overheard Booth discussing murder with his colleagues. A good agent might have realized that the actor was paying a suspicious amount of attention to where Mr. Lincoln might be found at any given time. And a clever investigator might have realized that an angry, disappointed southern rebel like John Wilkes Booth could be harboring a serious grudge against the president. But this time there was no policeman, no private investigator, no Allan Pinkerton to uncover the plot. Instead, Booth simply waited for the right opportunity. And it came.

On April 14, 1865—five days after the war had ended—the president went to the theater, and so did John Wilkes Booth.

As Mr. Lincoln sat enjoying the play, Booth slipped quietly into the flag-draped presidential box, aimed a six-inch brass gun at Lincoln's head, and pulled the trigger. Efforts to save the president's life were futile, and at 7:22 the next morning, Abraham Lincoln was pronounced dead.

Back in 1860, after his first election, the president had been troubled by a strange, haunting vision. In it he had seen himself with two faces: one pink and healthy; the other, deadly pale. At the time, Mrs. Lincoln had said this fantasy meant that he would be elected twice but would not live out his second term. Now, it seemed that that eerie prediction had come true.

Though Booth's bullet had ended the career of one of America's most important leaders, the young actor had not prevented the president from leaving his mark upon history. During his four years and five weeks in office, Lincoln had won the war, crushed the Confederacy, reunited the country, and pushed through the Thirteenth Amendment, which would soon outlaw slavery.

While he was a remarkable man in many ways, Abraham Lincoln was not perfect. Like all human beings, he made mistakes. Frederick Douglass noted that Lincoln had some of the "prejudices" of a "white man." The famous abolitionist felt that the president sometimes moved too slowly in the fight against slavery, and he thought Lincoln sometimes cared more about the survival of the Union than about Black freedom. Nonetheless, Mr. Douglass believed that—given the great political obstacles the president had to overcome—Abraham Lincoln's efforts to end slavery had truly been, "swift, zealous, radical, and determined."

Since his death, many have admired Lincoln. Some have criticized him. One thing, however, is certain. During his brief 213 weeks in office, the sixteenth president of the United States transformed the nation.

But things might have turned out differently. *If* Allan Pinkerton had not been on the job and *if* the Baltimore assassins had succeeded, Abraham Lincoln would never have been able to change U.S. history.

ꙮ Appendix ꙮ

For readers who would like to know about the other accomplishments and further adventures of some of the important characters mentioned in this book, here—in brief—are their stories.

John Wilkes Booth leaped from the presidential box onto the stage after shooting Lincoln. There, he shouted out the Latin motto of Virginia, *"Sic semper tyrannis"* ("Thus always to tyrants"), before escaping from Washington on horseback. After a huge manhunt, federal troops cornered him in a barn on a Virginia farm. Booth died there of a gunshot fired either by himself or a soldier.

Jefferson Davis argued constantly with his generals during the Civil War and never actually gave permission for General Lee's final surrender. After the war, he was captured by federal officials and imprisoned for two years before being released on bail. Davis, however, was never tried as a war criminal. After his release, he wrote a history of the Confederacy. The former Confederate president died in 1889.

Dorothea Dix volunteered to organize a nursing corps for the Union army soon after the start of the Civil War. Though she sometimes clashed with army doctors and administrators, Miss Dix ultimately became the superintendent of military nurses. Later, she continued her crusade for the better treatment of the mentally ill. Dorothea Dix died in 1887.

Frederick Douglass helped organize Black regiments during the Civil War and continued to demand civil rights for African Americans after the war ended. In 1877 he became marshal of the District of Columbia and later served as U.S. minister to Haiti. He died in 1895.

Samuel Felton continued to run his railroad, and the Philadelphia, Wilmington, and Baltimore line helped transport many Union troops during the Civil War. Later, he worked for several other railroads and supervised the building of Massachusetts's Hoosac Tunnel. He died in 1889.

Cypriano Ferrandini, Otis Hillard, and the other conspirators were never arrested by the federal government or questioned about their roles in the Baltimore Plot. Nothing is known about Hillard's further activities, but Ferrandini continued to cut hair in Baltimore until his death in 1910.

Hannibal Hamlin served one term as vice president. Hamlin—who was seldom consulted by Lincoln—said, unhappily, that during his term he felt as useless as a "fifth wheel on a coach." Hamlin was not nominated as Lincoln's running mate when the president ran for reelection in 1864, but during the Civil War, the former vice president served for a short time in the Union army. In 1869 the citizens of Maine once again elected him to the U.S. Senate, and subsequently he became the U.S. ambassador to Spain. Hamlin died on the Fourth of July 1891.

Norman Judd served as U.S. ambassador to Berlin from 1861 to 1865. After returning to the United States, he was elected to serve two terms in the U.S. Congress. He died in 1878.

Ward Hill Lamon served as a sort of self-appointed bodyguard to Mr. Lincoln and acted as the U.S. marshal of Washington, D.C. during Lincoln's presidency. He was away from the city, however, on the night Lincoln was assassinated. After the president's death, Lamon practiced law and wrote a controversial biography of Abraham Lincoln. He died in 1893.

Mary Todd Lincoln was devastated by the deaths of her husband and her sons Edward (who died in 1850), Willie (who died in 1862), and Tad (who died in 1871). Always an emotionally fragile woman, she was declared insane in 1875. Although that verdict was later reversed, she lived unhappily until her death in 1882.

Robert Todd Lincoln graduated from Harvard University and became a successful lawyer representing corporations and railroads. He also served as U.S. secretary of war under President James Garfield and was appointed ambassador to England by President Benjamin Harrison. He died in 1926.

Thomas (Tad) Lincoln had a speech defect and was often considered spoiled by his father's advisors, but bubbly, high-spirited Tad often cheered up his father during the hard war years. Sadly, he died of an illness in 1871 when he was only eighteen years old.

William (Willie) Lincoln was Tad's older brother who died of typhoid fever at age eleven in the White House, leaving both his parents devastated by grief.

Allan Pinkerton and his agents carried out many spy missions for the Union during the Civil War. Later, the detective and his operatives became known for helping to break up labor disputes and for tracking down famous criminals like Jesse James and Butch Cassidy. In his will Allan Pinkerton asked that some of his best agents—including Kate Warne—be buried near his grave. Today, the detective agency he founded is still a successful security business. Allan Pinkerton died in 1884.

General Winfield Scott retired from his post as Commanding General of the U.S. Army soon after the outbreak of the Civil War. He died in 1866.

Frederick Seward followed his father, William Seward, into politics and served as an assistant secretary of state. He received an almost fatal head wound when one of John Wilkes Booth's co-conspirators tried to assassinate his father. Fortunately, Frederick recovered and lived until 1915.

William H. Seward was almost killed by one of Booth's co-conspirators on the night Lincoln was assassinated. Although badly wounded, Seward survived and continued to act as secretary of state for Lincoln's successor, President Andrew Johnson. In 1867, Seward became famous for buying what is now the state of Alaska from Russia. At the time many people mocked the purchase of a vast, frozen wilderness, calling Alaska "Seward's Folly." Now, however, many are grateful for the huge amounts of oil and natural gas that Alaska sends to the rest of the country. Seward died in 1872.

Kate Warne became superintendent of Pinkerton's Female Detective Bureau and helped Pinkerton spy for the Union during the Civil War. Her career, however, was cut short by illness; and she died in 1868 at the age of thirty-five with Allan Pinkerton beside her.

ὃ Notes, Sources, and Further Reading ὅ

Although, to my knowledge, there are no other books specifically dealing with the Baltimore Plot for young readers, two excellent adult books (Daniel Stashower's *The Hour of Peril* and Michael Kline's *The Baltimore Plot*) do exist. Those who want even more information might also explore some of the published primary sources I have used. These include Pinkerton's own written memoir of the case in *The Baltimore Lincoln Assassination Plot and Other Civil War Secrets*, the original accounts and letters collected by Pinkerton in his book *History and Evidence of the Passage of Abraham Lincoln from Harrisburg, PA, to Washington, D.C., on the 22d and 23d of February, 1861,* the original reports of Pinkerton and his detectives published in Norma B. Cuthbert's *Lincoln and the Baltimore Plot, 1861: From Pinkerton Records and Related Papers,* and Lincoln's original speeches published in William Turner Coggeshall's *The Journeys of Abraham Lincoln: From Springfield to Washington, 1861 as President Elect and from Washington to Springfield, 1865, as President Martyred.*

Although there are many fine books about Abraham Lincoln for younger readers, Russell Freedman's *Lincoln: A Photobiography* is one of my personal favorites. Movie lovers might enjoy the adult film *Lincoln* (directed by Steven Spielberg), which deals with Lincoln's struggle to end the war and abolish slavery in the last months of his life, and those interested in the Civil War might find Ken Burns's adult documentary on the subject fascinating.

Readers should also know that all quotations used in this book, unless otherwise noted, retain the spelling and punctuation of the original—even though it may differ from modern usage. In order to save space, titles of some works have been abbreviated in the following source notes, and since most young readers are unfamiliar with such academic terms as "ibid." and "op. cit.," I have deliberately refrained from using them here.

Chapter 1: "What Does Anyone Want to Harm Me For?"

"Mary, we are elected": Sandburg, p. 182.

"responsibility that was upon . . .": Donald, pp. 255–56, quoting Lincoln's description of his election night.

"sick of office-holding . . .": Herndon, p. 484, quoting a conversation he had with Lincoln shortly after the election.

"are created equal . . . Life, Liberty . . .": See "Declaration of Independence: A Transcript" listed under Online Sources.

"Positive Good": Striner, p. 22, quoting the title of a famous, extremely racist speech given in 1837 by southern statesman John C. Calhoun in which he claimed that slavery was beneficial to both whites and Blacks.

"monstrous injustice": Donald, p. 176, quoting a statement made by Lincoln during his debates with political rival Stephen Douglas.

"the evil out of which all other . . .": Cooper, p. 81, quoting a statement made by Lincoln to his minister in Springfield.

"If slavery is not wrong . . .": Oates, p. 75.

"ill-bred, profane . . .": Zall, p. xviii.

"jackass": Donald, p. 280.

"half-slave . . .": Donald, p. 206.

"Let-us . . . remember . . .": Sandburg, p. 188.

"his feet chained . . .": Goodwin, p. 306, quoting the nineteenth-century journalist Henry Villard.

"They'll kill ye . . .": Sandburg, p. 185.

"something would happen": Donald, p. 271.

"all imagination": Stashower, p. 2.

"Trust in the Lord . . .": Donald, p. 271.

"unimpassioned reason": Achorn, p. 86.

"What does anyone want . . .": Stashower, p. 2.

"I can be turned out . . .": Coggeshall, p. 42, quoting a speech given by Lincoln during his journey to Washington.

Chapter 2: Mr. Pinkerton Takes the Case

"a matter of great importance": Pinkerton,
  The Baltimore Lincoln Assassination Plot, p. 25.

six men who'd dared to vote for him . . . : Information in this
  paragraph comes from Kline, pp. 10–11. It is important to
  remember that in 1860, women could not vote and ballots
  often were not secret.

"vast moral evil": Lincoln quoted in Oates, p. 71.

Chapter 3: A Visit to Mobtown

"no d—d abolitionist . . .": Pinkerton, *The Baltimore Lincoln
  Assassination Plot*, p. 27.

"daring": Pinkerton, *The Baltimore Lincoln Assassination Plot*,
  p. 27.

"attempted violence . . . disposition to resort . . .": Pinkerton,
  The Baltimore Assassination Plot, p. 27.

"the gutters flowed . . .": Stashower, p. 101, quoting a
  contemporary account in *The Baltimore Republican*.

"cut and bruised...nearly knocked out . . .": All quotations
  in this paragraph come from Silberman p. 46, quoting
  Frederick Douglass.

John H. Hutcheson: This name is spelled both as "Hutchinson"
  and "Hutcheson" in the original Pinkerton records in
  Cuthbert. For the sake of clarity, I have chosen one spelling
  and used it throughout.

"worm out secrets . . .": Mackay, p. 74, quoting Pinkerton's
  description of his first meeting with Kate Warne.

Chapter 4: "I Bid You an Affectionate Farewell."

"A. Lincoln, White House . . .": Stashower, p. 133.

"sainted . . . idolized": Holzer, p. 29.

"Love is eternal": Sandburg, p. 78.

"pale . . . quivered with emotion": Kline, p. 39, quoting the
  impressions of a contemporary journalist.

"My friends . . . No one . . .": Sandburg, pp. 195–96.

"We will pray for you": Kline, p. 45.

"do good to those who hate you . . .": Holzer, p. 33.

Chapter 5: "Both Sexes and All Ages Are for War."

"Both sexes . . .": Sandburg, p. 238, quoting the *London Times*.

"every drop of my blood": William C. Davis, p. 304.

"war, long and bloody": William C. Davis, p. 304.

Chapter 6: Gone!

"For those who like . . .": Zall, p. xiii.

"magnificent welcome": All quotations in this paragraph from Coggeshall, p. 25.

"generous support": Coggeshall, p. 25.

"keep silence": Coggeshall, p. 25.

Just plain gone: Although some accounts say the incident with the satchel took place while Lincoln was in Pennsylvania, I have followed Stashower's lead in believing that it occurred in Indianapolis.

"free, happy, and unrestrained . . .": Holzer, p. 32, quoting a statement made by Mrs. Lincoln in an interview with Lincoln's law partner and biographer, William Herndon.

"killed": Stashower, p. 150, quoting a letter written by John Nicolay.

Chapter 7: "I Would Like to Tell You, But I Dare Not."

"I am informed . . .": Pinkerton, *The Baltimore Lincoln Assassination Plot*, p. 31.

"that reminds me . . .": All quotations from the conversation between Davies and Hillard in this chapter come from Davies's original report in Cuthbert, pp. 29–30.

"I have a message of importance . . .": Pinkerton's dispatch, reproduced in Cuthbert, p. 25.

Chapter 8: Waiting for News

"I have a message of importance . . .": Pinkerton's dispatch, reproduced in Cuthbert, p. 25.

"At Columbus . . .": Judd's response to Pinkerton, reproduced in Cuthbert, p. 25.

"'the President' . . .": Coggeshall, p. 28.

"The American Union, forever": Coggeshall, p. 30.

"A union that nothing can sever": Coggeshall, p. 30.

"our national difficulties will . . . pass away": Coggeshall, p. 33.

"forgotten and blown . . .": Coggeshall, p. 33.

Chapter 9: Decisions

"there was a plot on foot . . .": Letter dated November 3, 1869, from Judd to Pinkerton in Pinkerton, *History and Evidence*, p. 13.

"very much obliged . . .": From William Scott's report, reproduced in Cuthbert, p. 31.

"I think not": From William Scott's report, reproduced in Cuthbert, p. 31.

"causing undue anxiety . . .": Pinkerton, *The Baltimore Lincoln Assassination Plot*, p. 47.

"lashed to the muzzle . . .": Stashower, p. 167.

"clear . . . strong": "John Cabell Breckinridge, 14th Vice President (1857–1861)."

"Abraham Lincoln of Illinois . . .": Stashower, pp. 167–68.

"The votes were counted . . .": Kline, p. 102.

"packed together . . .": Coggeshall, p. 37.

"frantic enthusiasm": Coggeshall, p. 41.

"Citizens of Ohio . . .": Coggeshall, p. 39.

"Nothing going wrong . . .": Stashower, p. 170, quoting *The New York Herald*.

"densely populated . . . food for the sword . . .": Kline, p. 122.

"What a pity . . .": Stashower, p. 168, quoting a statement Hillard made to Pinkerton agent Davies.

Chapter 10: "Lincoln Shall Die in This City."

"He may pass through . . .": From Pinkerton's report of this conversation, reproduced in Cuthbert, p. 34.

"Oh . . . that is easily . . . ": From Pinkerton's report of this conversation reproduced in Cuthbert, p. 34.

"best manner . . . Southern rights": From Pinkerton's report of this conversation, reproduced in Cuthbert, p. 35.

Ferrandini: In Pinkerton's original notes, this name is spelled as "Ferrandina." Ferrandini is the form used in all modern accounts.

"true friend to the South": From Pinkerton's report, reproduced in Cuthbert, p. 35.

"his eyes fairly . . . glistened . . .": From Pinkerton's report, reproduced in Cuthbert, pp. 36–37.

"faces . . . eagerly turned . . .": Pinkerton, *The Baltimore Lincoln Assassination Plot,* p. 37.

"strange power": From Pinkerton's report, reproduced in Cuthbert, p. 37.

"Murder of any kind . . .": From Pinkerton's report, reproduced in Cuthbert, p. 37.

"Never, never . . .": From Pinkerton's report, reproduced in Cuthbert, p. 37.

"Traitor": From Pinkerton's report, reproduced in Cuthbert, p. 37.

"save": From Pinkerton's report, reproduced in Cuthbert, p. 37.

"If I alone must do it . . .": From Pinkerton's report, reproduced in Cuthbert, p. 37.

Chapter 11: "There Is No Crisis."

"Abe . . . They say . . .": All quotations from the conversation between Lincoln, the miner, and Ellsworth come from Stashower, p. 171.

"good natured, kindly . . .": Stashower, p. 173.

"frivolous and uncertain": Stashower, p. 173.

"If I had another face . . .": Boller, p. 125.

"give this subject . . .": Coggeshall, p. 43.

"There is no crisis . . .": Coggeshall, p. 44.

"he had always found it very difficult . . .": Donald, p. 275.

Chapter 12: A Sitting Duck

"Oh! That is easily promised . . .": From Pinkerton's report, reproduced in Cuthbert, p. 34.

"entire police force . . . in full sympathy . . .": Pinkerton, *The Baltimore Lincoln Assassination Plot,* pp. 36–37.

"a Police Escort": Kline, p. 120.

Chapter 13: "Our Separation from the Old Union Is Complete."

"Our separation from the old Union . . .": Cooper, p. 190.

"smell Southern [gun]powder. . .": Stashower, p. 181.

"clear": William C. Davis, p. 307.

"wrong": Jefferson Davis, p. 201.

"the suffering of millions": Jefferson Davis, p. 202.

"folly and wickedness": Jefferson Davis, p. 202.

"needlessly": Jefferson Davis, p. 201.

"well-instructed and disciplined": Jefferson Davis, p. 202.

"honor and security": Jefferson Davis, p. 201.

"the God of our fathers": All quotations in this paragraph from Jefferson Davis, p. 203.

Chapter 14: A Clear-Cut Sign of Trouble

"the long and the short . . .": Zall, p. 16.

"I have come to see you . . .": Zall, p. 16.

"story teller and . . . joke maker": Stashower, p. 182, quoting *The New York Herald.*

"Some three months ago . . .": All quotations from the incident with Grace Bedell are from Kline, p. 116. Note that the original punctuation has been altered in order to provide clarity.

"had to struggle . . .": Stashower, p. 182, quoting the nineteenth-century journalist Henry Villard.

"women fainted . . .": Stashower, p. 183, quoting New York's *Commercial Advertiser.*

"the pressure was so great . . .": Stashower, p. 182, quoting the nineteenth-century journalist Henry Villard.

"grand reception": Coggeshall, p. 50.

"Show us the Rail Splitter": All quotations in this paragraph are from Kline, p. 139, quoting the Albany *Atlas and Argus.*

"inadvisable": All quotations in this paragraph are from a letter written by the Baltimore Republican Party Committee that is quoted in Kline, pp. 142–43.

"evidence . . . was accumulating": Stashower, p. 187.

Chapter 15: Eight Red Cards

"sober . . . what is the matter with you?": All quotations from the following dialogue between Hillard and Davies are taken from Davies's report, reproduced in Cuthbert, pp. 46–48.

"joyfully informed": Pinkerton, *The Baltimore Lincoln Assassination Plot,* p. 48.

"strangely silent": Pinkerton, *The Baltimore Lincoln Assassination Plot,* p. 48.

"dense, excited": All quotations in this paragraph are from Pinkerton, *The Baltimore Lincoln Assassination Plot,* p. 49.

"the nation of the foul . . .": Pinkerton, *The Baltimore Lincoln Assassination Plot,* p.50.

"I resolved . . .": Pinkerton, *The Baltimore Lincoln Assassination Plot,* p. 51.

Chapter 16: A Message for Mr. Judd

"never let me down": Mackay, p. 74.

"vast . . . silent": Kline, p. 154, quoting the poet Walt Whitman's description of Lincoln's arrival in New York.

"Honor to a President . . . The American Union, forever": Coggeshall, p. 30.

"Welcome, Abraham Lincoln . . .": Kline, p. 153.

"very pale and fatigued": From Kate Warne's report, reproduced in Cuthbert, p. 41.

"immediately": From Kate Warne's report, reproduced in Cuthbert, p. 41.

Chapter 17: Ten-to-One Odds

"Mr. Judd, I presume . . . Yes madam": Letter from Judd to Pinkerton, November 3, 1867, published in Pinkerton, *History and Evidence,* p. 14.

Upset and obviously unsure: My description of this event is derived from Kate Warne's report, reproduced in Cuthbert, pp. 41–43.

"keep cool": From Kate Warne's report, reproduced in Cuthbert, p. 42.

"tickled to death": From Kate Warne's report, reproduced in Cuthbert, p. 45.

"tired": From Kate Warne's report, reproduced in Cuthbert, p. 45.

"There is nothing . . .": Kline, p. 167.

"I have been told I look like you . . . You do look . . .": This exchange is quoted in Kline, p. 168.

"mutually surpass . . .": Kline, p. 168.

"Ball of hair . . .": Harris, p. 165.

"Great Grizzly Mammoth Bear Samson": Stashower, p. 213.

"I don't know that I can manage . . .": Stashower, p. 213.

"derrick and a windmill": Zall, p. xii.

"the Undertaker of the Union": Sandburg, p. 201.

Chapter 18: "Find Mr. Lincoln."

"Old Fuss and Feathers": Kline, p. 19.

"touched [him] on the elbow": Seward, p. 508.

"General Scott is impressed": Seward, p. 509.

Chapter 19: "I Fully Appreciate These Suggestions."

"I shall do all that may be in my power . . .": Coggeshall, p. 56.

"wild mass of human beings": Stashower, p. 227, quoting an article in *The Philadelphia Inquirer.*

"cool, calm, and collected": Letter from Pinkerton to Herndon, August 23, 1866, reproduced in Cuthbert, p. 11.

"If you follow the course suggested . . .": Letter from Judd to Pinkerton, November 3, 1867, reproduced in Pinkerton, *History and Evidence,* p. 16.

"I fully appreciate . . .": Pinkerton, *The Baltimore Lincoln Assassination Plot,* p. 55.

Chapter 20: "I Shall Think It over Carefully."

All quotations in this chapter come from Seward, pp. 509–10.

Chapter 21: So What Could Go Wrong?

No quotations in this chapter.

Chapter 22: "One of the Thousand Threats Against You"

"all men are created equal . . . unalienable . . . Life, Liberty . . .": All these quotations are from the Declaration of Independence. See "Declaration of Independence: A Transcription" under Online Sources. Readers should note that at the time the Declaration was written and at the time Abraham Lincoln lived, it was customary to refer to "all men" when the speaker actually meant "all people."

"I have never had a feeling . . .": All quotations in this paragraph are from Coggeshall, p. 58.

"sent by his father . . .": All quotations in this paragraph come from Herndon's interview with Judd, November 18, 1866, reproduced in Cuthbert, p. 111.

"Dear Sir": Kline, p. 217, quoting a letter found in Lincoln's papers.

Chapter 23: The Mob Wants Blood

"no damned Abolitionist . . .": Kline, p. 229, quoting an 1899 biography of Hamlin.

Chapter 24: "What Is Your Own Judgment upon This Matter?"

"preserve the peace . . .": Kline, p. 219.

"d—d piece of cowardice": From Herndon's interview with Judd, 1866, reproduced in Cuthbert, p. 112.

"Well, Mr. Lincoln . . .": Letter from Judd to Pinkerton, November 3, 1867, reproduced in Pinkerton, *History and Evidence,* p. 19.

"your life is not safe . . .": Kline, p. 42, quoting Horace Greeley, the famous editor of the *New-York Tribune.*

"I have thought over . . .": Letter from Judd to Pinkerton, November 3, 1867, reproduced in Pinkerton, *History and Evidence,* p. 19.

"that settles the matter . . .": Letter from Judd to Pinkerton, November 3, 1867, reproduced in Pinkerton, *History and Evidence,* p. 19.

"danger or no danger": Kline, p. 45, quoting the nineteenth-century journalist Henry Villard.

"never in his life . . .": This information comes from Lincoln's own recollection of events as reproduced in Cuthbert, p. xvi.

Chapter 25: "Where Is Nuts?"

"Where is Nuts?": From Pinkerton's report, reproduced in Cuthbert, p. 76.

"Nuts left at six . . .": From Pinkerton's report, reproduced in Cuthbert, p. 77.

" if fighting had to be done . . .": From Pinkerton's report, reproduced in Cuthbert, p. 79.

"would work right": From Pinkerton's report, reproduced in Cuthbert, p. 79.

Chapter 26: Dread and Danger

"We are getting along . . .": Pinkerton's 1866 account in Cuthbert, p. 16.

"as full of fun . . .": From Pinkerton's report, reproduced in Cuthbert, p. 81.

"I wish I was in the land of cotton . . .": Meacham and McGraw, p. 81.

"No doubt there will be . . .": Pinkerton, *The Baltimore Lincoln Assassination Plot*, p. 65.

Chapter 27: "Highly Important News"

"well-to-do . . . farmer": Kline, p. 263, quoting Elihu Washburne's description of meeting Lincoln at the station.

"Abe, you can't . . .": From Pinkerton's report, reproduced in Cuthbert, p. 82.

"Don't strike him . . .": From Pinkerton's report, reproduced in Cuthbert, p. 82.

"Trot him out . . .": All quotations from the crowd taken from the *New York Times* report extensively quoted in Kline, p. 285.

"Mrs. Lincoln and the boys got off . . .": Although most accounts say that the Lincoln family was not directly accosted by the mob, the *New York Times* report says that some members of the mob invaded Mrs. Lincoln's compartment and had to be pushed out. Since other sources dispute this, it's possible that the *Times* account is a mistake or an exaggeration.

"HIGHLY IMPORTANT NEWS . . .": The *New York Times*, February 25, 1861, p. 1.

"lunatic": Kline, p. 309.

"wanting in pluck": Stashower, p. 263.

"thief in the night": Stashower, p. 263.

"twenty picked men . . .": All quotations in this paragraph from Pinkerton's report, reproduced in Cuthbert, p. 89.

"I did not then . . .": Lincoln's statement to his friend Isaac N. Arnold, in Cuthbert, p. xvi.

Chapter 28: The President Speaks

"high-pitched": Oates, p. 39.

"one section of our country . . .": Coggeshall, p. 68.

"lawful right": Coggeshall, p. 63.

"perpetual": Coggeshall, p. 65.

"No state, upon its own . . .": Coggeshall, p. 65.

"preserve, protect . . .": Coggeshall, p. 70.
In this section of his speech Lincoln is quoting the U.S. presidential oath of office.

"most solemn": Coggeshall, p. 70.

"We are not enemies . . .": All quotations in this paragraph from Coggeshall, p. 70.

"I do solemnly swear . . .": The presidential oath of office as stated in the U.S. Constitution Article II, Section 1, Clause 8 from "Constitution Annotated" listed in Online Sources.

"hurrahed": "The New Administration," *The New York Times,* March 5, 1861, p. 1.

"declaration of war": Cooper, p. 216, quoting the southerner Howell Cobb.

"the foul withering...": Goodwin, p. 331, quoting Frederick Douglass.

"strong, straightforward . . .": Donald, p. 284, quoting the Indianapolis *Daily Journal.*

"rambling . . . loose-jointed": Donald, p. 284, quoting the Albany *Atlas and Argus.*

"stupid, ambiguous . . .": Detzer, p. 213, quoting a passage in the southerner Emma Holmes's diary.

Chapter 29: "If This Must Be Done, *I* Must Do It."

restless: See Goodwin's description, p. 335.

"maintain the authority of the [U.S.] Government": Donald, p. 287, quoting Postmaster-General Montgomery Blair.

"If this must be done . . .": Donald, p. 290.

"in the dumps": Donald, p. 288, quoting Lincoln.

"keeled over": Klein, p. 358, quoting Mary Lincoln.

"Of all the trials . . .": Goodwin, p. 340.

"Wanted—A Policy . . .": The New York Times, April 3, 1861.

"demoralizing, disorganizing . . .": Sandburg, p. 227, quoting *The New York Herald.*

"this uncertain state . . .": McClintock, p. 245, quoting the abolitionist and loyal Lincoln supporter Carl Schurz.

"supply Fort Sumter": All quotations in this paragraph are from Lincoln's message to the Confederate government, reproduced in Cooper, p. 261.

"suicide": William C. Davis, p. 323, quoting Robert Toombs.

"a civil war greater . . .": Sandburg, p. 229.

"I am ordered . . .": Sandburg, p. 229.

"Loyal citizens": Sandburg, p. 230, quoting Lincoln's call for troops.

"the honor, integrity . . .": Cooper, p. 270, quoting Lincoln's call for troops.

"cowardly . . . rascals": Klein, p. 424, quoting statements heard by William Russell, a correspondent for the *London Times,* in Charleston just after the fall of Fort Sumter.

Chapter 30: "Forever Free"

slavery, not secession: Lincoln makes this clear in his second inaugural address, quoted in Coggeshall, p. 72.

"every drop of blood": Coggeshall, p. 73, quoting Lincoln's second inaugural address.

"half-slave and half-free . . . all one thing . . .": Donald, p. 206.

"conceived in Liberty . . .": Lincoln, The Gettysburg Address, quoted in Sandburg, p. 444.

"one of the most meritorious . . .": Goodwin, p. 650, quoting Lincoln.

"one gentleman . . .": Goodwin, p. 553, quoting Douglass.

"freely": Goodwin, p. 207, quoting Douglass.

"feel for a moment . . .": Goodwin, p. 650, quoting Douglass.

"I, Abraham Lincoln . . .": Striner, pp. 181–82.

"We shout for joy . . .": Goodwin, p. 483.

"I never in my life . . .": Goodwin, p. 499.

"reject the emancipation Proclamation": Guelzo, p. 213.

"bloody, barbarous . . .": Guelzo, p. 211.

"abolitionist faction": Oates, p. 115, quoting sentiments held by some anti-Lincoln Midwest Democrats.

"tyrant": Striner, p. 194, quoting northern Democrats who opposed Lincoln and the Emancipation Proclamation.

"My word is out . . .": Goodwin, p. 483.

"the greatest wrong . . .": Goodwin, p. 469.

"the millions now in bondage . . .": Goodwin, p. 687.

"land in the seventh . . .": Achorn, p. xviii, quoting a Confederate officer.

"The Year of Jubilee . . .": These words appear on the photograph of a flyer in Catton and Ketchum, p. 585.

"Dear Husband . . . more cheerful": This exchange between Mr. and Mrs. Lincoln was quoted in Goodwin, p. 733.

"never be glad again": Achorn, p. 85, quoting a remark made by Lincoln to a friend.

"soul, life, and possessions . . .": Oates, p. 155.

"formed for the white . . .": Oates, p. 155.

"decisive and great": Goodwin, p. 728, quoting Booth's diary.

"prejudices . . . white man": Meacham and McGraw, p. 91, quoting Douglass.

"swift, zealous, radical . . .": Meacham and McGraw, p. 91, quoting Douglass.

Appendix

"fifth wheel on a coach": See "Hamlin, Hannibal (1809–1891)" in Online Sources.

Bibliography

Books

Achorn, Edward. *Every Drop of Blood: The Momentous Second Inauguration of Abraham Lincoln*. New York: Atlantic Monthly Press, 2020.

Boller, Paul F., Jr. *Presidential Anecdotes*. Rev. ed. New York: Oxford University Press, 1996.

Brown, Thomas J. *Dorothea Dix: New England Reformer*. Cambridge, MA: Harvard University Press, 1998.

Catton, Bruce. *The Civil War*. New York: The Fairfax Press, 1980.

Catton, Bruce (narrative) and Richard M. Ketchum et al., eds. *The American Heritage Picture History of the Civil War*. New York: American Heritage Publishing Co., 1960.

Coggeshall, William Turner. *The Journeys of Abraham Lincoln: From Springfield to Washington, 1861 as President Elect and from Washington to Springfield, 1865, as President Martyred*. Dover, OH: Old Hundredth Press, 2008.

Cooper, William J. *We Have the War Upon Us: The Onset of the Civil War, November 1860–April 1861*. New York: Knopf, 2012.

Cuthbert, Norma B., ed. *Lincoln and the Baltimore Plot, 1861: From Pinkerton Records and Related Papers*. San Marino, CA: The Huntington Library, 1949.

Davis, Jefferson. *The Rise and Fall of the Confederate Government: Volume 1*. Foreword by James M. McPherson. Boston: Da Capo Press, 1990.

Davis, William C. *Jefferson Davis: The Man and His Hour*. Baton Rouge: Louisiana State University Press, 1991.

Detzer, David. *Allegiance: Fort Sumter, Charleston, and the Beginning of the Civil War*. San Diego: Harcourt, 2001.

Donald, David Herbert. *Lincoln*. New York: Simon & Schuster, 1995.

Goodwin, Doris Kearns. *Team of Rivals: The Political Genius of Abraham Lincoln*. New York: Simon & Schuster, 2005.

Guelzo, Allen C. *Lincoln's Emancipation Proclamation: The End of Slavery in America*. New York: Simon & Schuster, 2004.

Harris, Neil. *Humbug: The Art of P. T. Barnum*. Boston: Little, Brown, 1973.

Herndon, William H., and Jesse William Weik. *Herndon's Lincoln: A True Story of a Great Life*. New York: Cosmo Classics, 2009.

Holzer, Harold. *Lincoln as I Knew Him: Gossip, Tributes, and Revelations from His Best Friends and Worst Enemies.* Chapel Hill, NC: Algonquin Books of Chapel Hill, 1999.

Jackson, Kenneth T., ed. *The Encyclopedia of New York City.* New Haven, CT: Yale University Press, and New York: The New-York Historical Society, 1995.

Klein, Maury. *Days of Defiance: Sumter, Secession, and the Coming of the Civil War.* New York: Random House, 1997.

Kline, Michael J. *The Baltimore Plot: The First Conspiracy to Assassinate Abraham Lincoln.* Yadley, PA: Westholme, 2008.

Mackay, James. *Allan Pinkerton: The First Private Eye.* New York: John Wiley, 1996.

McClintock, Russell. *Lincoln and the Decision for War: The Northern Response to Secession.* Chapel Hill: University of North Carolina Press, 2008.

Meacham, Jon, and Tim McGraw. *Songs of America: Patriotism, Protest, and the Music That Made a Nation.* New York: Random House, 2019.

Oates, Stephen B. *Abraham Lincoln: The Man Behind the Myths.* New York: Harper & Row, 1984.

Pinkerton, Allan. *History and Evidence of the Passage of Abraham Lincoln from Harrisburg, PA, to Washington, D.C., on the 22d and 23d of February, 1861.* Reproduced by Cornell Library Digital Collections, n.d.

Pinkerton, Allan. *The Baltimore Lincoln Assassination Plot and Other Civil War Secrets.* Publisher of One, Baltimore, MD, n.d.

Potter, David M. *The Impending Crisis: America Before the Civil War: 1848–1861.* New York: HarperCollins, 2011.

Sandburg, Carl. *Abraham Lincoln: The Prairie Years and the War Years.* New York: Harcourt Brace, 1954.

Seward, Frederick W. *Seward at Washington, as Senator and Secretary of State: A Memoir of His Life, with Selections from His Letters, 1846–1861.* London: Forgotten Books, 2018.

Silberman, Lauren R. *Wicked Baltimore: Charm City Sin and Scandal.* Charleston, SC: The History Press, 2011.

Stashower, Daniel. *The Hour of Peril: The Secret Plot to Murder Lincoln Before the Civil War.* New York: Minotaur Press, 2013.

Striner, Richard. *Father Abraham: Lincoln's Relentless Struggle to End Slavery.* Oxford, UK: Oxford University Press, 2006.

Tiffany, Francis. *Life of Dorothea Lynde Dix.* London: Forgotten Books, 2012.

Zall, Paul M., ed. *Abe Lincoln's Legacy of Laughter: Humorous Stories by and about Abraham Lincoln.* Knoxville: University of Tennessee Press, 2007.

Newspapers

The New York Times

Online Sources

"Constitution Annotated," www.constitution.congress.gov.

"Declaration of Independence: A Transcription," National Archives, www.archives.gov/founding-docs/declaration-transcript.

Felton Family Papers, Collection 1151, Historical Society of Pennsylvania, www2.hsp.org/collections/manuscripts/f/Felton1151.html.

Ford, Martin. "Gangs of Baltimore." *Humanities* 29, no. 3 (May/June 2008).

"Hamlin, Hannibal (1809–1891)," Biographical Directory of the United States Congress, 1774–Present, https://bioguideretro.congress.gov/Home/MemberDetails?memIndex=h000121.

"History: Lincoln and His Marshal," U.S. Marshals Service, www.usmarshals.gov/history/lincoln/lincoln_and_his_marshal.htm.

"John Cabell Breckinridge, 14th Vice President (1857–1861)," United States Senate, www.senate.gov/about/officers-staff/vice-president/VP_John_Breckinridge.htm.

"Judd, Norman Buel (1815–1878)," Biographical Directory of the United States Congress, 1774–Present, https://bioguideretro.congress.gov/Home/MemberDetails?memIndex=J000277.

"13th Amendment to the Constitution of the United States," National Museum of African American History & Culture, www.nmaahc.si.edu/blog-post/13th-amendment-constitution-united-states.

Villard, Henry. "Recollections of Lincoln." *The Atlantic*, Special Commemerative Issue Feb. 2012. http://www.theatlantic.com/magazine/archive/2012/02/recollections-of-lincoln/308796/.

"Ward Hill Lamon," www.tulane.edu/~sumter/Lamon.html.

Watts, Dale E. "How Bloody Was Bleeding Kansas?" *Kansas History: A Journal of the Central Plains* 18, no.2 (Summer 1995): 116–29, www.kshs.org/publicat/history/1995summer_watts.pdf.

❧ Index ❧